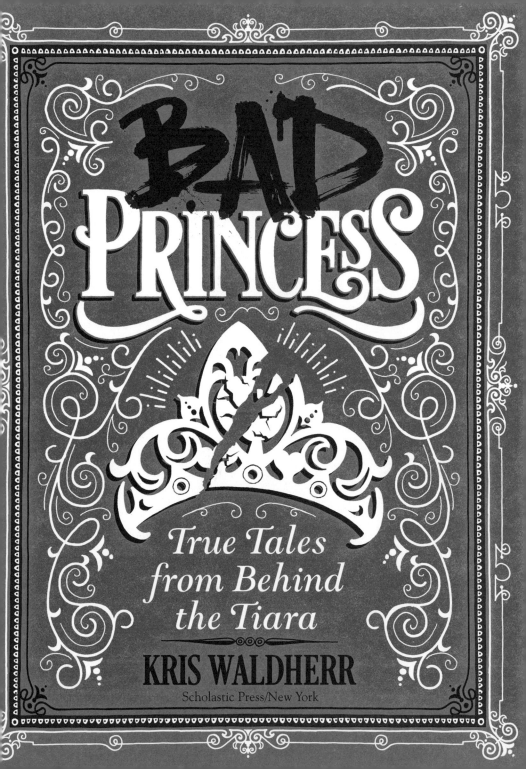

BAD PRINCESS

True Tales from Behind the Tiara

KRIS WALDHERR

Scholastic Press/New York

FOR MY DAUGHTER, THEA, WITH LOVE

Photos ©: 15: Marzolino/Shutterstock; 22: Image Asset Management/age fotostock; 27: Elizabeth Báthory (oil on canvas), Unknown Artist, (17th century)/Private Collection/Photo © PVDE/Bridgeman Images; 36 top right: PAINTING/Alamy Images; 36 center: De Agostini Picture L/age fotostock; 36 bottom left: Ann Ronan Pictures/age fotostock; 36 bottom right: Bettmann/Getty Images; 37 top: GeorgiosArt/iStockphoto; 37 center top: Everett Historical/Shutterstock; 37 center bottom: Print Collector/Getty Images; 37 bottom: World History Archive/Ann Ronan Collection/age fotostock; 40 left: The Print Collector/age fotostock; 40 right: The Print Collector/Alamy Images; 42: Everett-Art/Shutterstock; 44 background: Photos.com/Thinkstock; 44 top, 44 center left: Portrait of Françoise-Marie de Bourbon (1677–1749) and Louise-Françoise de Bourbon (1673 –1743) (oil on canvas), Vignon, Philippe (1638 –1701)/Château de Versailles, France/Bridgeman Images; 44 center: Everett-Art/Shutterstock; 44 center right: Fine Art Images/age fotostock; 44 center bottom right: Marie-Anne de Bourbon (1666 –1739) Princess of Conti (oil on canvas), Largilliere, Nicholas de (1656 –1746) (attr. to)/Musée des Augustins, Toulouse, France/Bridgeman Images; 44 bottom left: Fine Art Images/age fotostock; 44 bottom right: De Agostini Picture Library/age fotostock; 46: Portrait of Françoise-Marie de Bourbon (1677–1749) and Louise-Françoise de Bourbon (1673 –1743) (oil on canvas), Vignon, Philippe (1638 –1701)/Château de Versailles, France/Bridgeman Images; 53: Mary Evans Picture Library/age fotostock; 59: Library of Congress; 61: Princess Caraboo of Javasu (Mary Baker), 1817 (oil on panel), Bird, Edward (1772 –1819)/Bristol Museum and Art Gallery, UK/Civic painting, transferred 1972./Bridgeman Images; 64 top: De Agostini/G. Dagli Orti/Getty Images; 64 center right: Image Asset Management/age fotostock; 64 center left: Elizabeth Báthory (oil on canvas), Unknown Artist, (17th century)/ Private Collection/Photo © PVDE/Bridgeman Images; 64 center bottom right: Fine Art Images/age fotostock; 64 bottom: Library of Congress; 70 top right: Library of Congress; 70 center right: Library of Congress; 70 bottom left: Library of Congress; 71 top right: Library of Congress; 71 center left: Library of Congress; 72: The Prince of Wales/British Library, London, UK/© British Library Board. All Rights Reserved/Bridgeman Images; 74: Photos.com/Thinkstock; 78: Library of Congress; 82: Library of Congress; 92: Library of Congress; 96: Arnoldo Mondadori Editore S.P./age fotostock; 98: Library of Congress; 99: Wikimedia; 105: Rex Features/AP Images; 108: Mondadori Portfolio/Getty Images; 110 top center: Fine Art Images/age fotostock; 110 top right: Library of Congress; 110 center: De Agostini/G. Dagli Orti/Getty Images; 110 center right: Library of Congress; 111 top far left: De Agostini/G. Dagli Orti/Getty Images; 111 top left: Elizabeth Báthory (oil on canvas), Unknown Artist, (17th century)/Private Collection/Photo © PVDE/Bridgeman Images; 111 top center: Marzolino/Shutterstock; 111 center: PHAS/Getty Images; 111 bottom: Newspix/Getty Images; 119 bottom: Pascal Le Segretain/Getty Images; 120 top: Osports/Getty Images; 120 center: Bridow/WENN.com/age fotostock; 120 bottom: Carlos Chavez/Getty Images; 122 center: Guildhall Library & Art Gallery/age fotostock; 122 bottom: jorisvo/Shutterstock; 123 top: Popperfoto/Getty Images; 123 bottom: Marzolino/Shutterstock.

Library of Congress Cataloging-in-Publication Data available

ISBN 978-1-338-04798-1

10 9 8 7 6 5 4 3 2 1   18 19 20 21 22

Printed in the U.S.A.   23

First edition, January 2018

Cover design by Maeve Norton
Book design by Kris Waldherr and Kay Petronio

Table of Contents

DWARFS. A princess-in-distress's best hope for survival.

INTRODUCTION:
Once Upon a Time

> "It's only in fairy tales that princesses can afford to wait for the handsome prince to save them."
>
> — Meg Cabot, *Abandon* (2011)

nyone familiar with fairy tales knows that most princesses lead dangerous, desperate lives. Behind the fluffy gowns and diamond tiaras, there's usually an enemy lurking in the shadows. Snow White's evil stepmother plots to have the princess killed when Snow becomes fairest in the land. Sleeping Beauty is cursed to drop dead once she turns sixteen. And in real life, the tragic death of Great Britain's Princess Diana in a car accident showed that not all princesses live happily ever after.

Despite all this, many of us grow up yearning to become a princess. From the moment a little girl is born, it seems she can't escape this princess obsession.

THE PRINCESS RULES

For many, the word "princess" implies more than just being a king's daughter or a prince's bride. What makes a princess special? Here are a few "rules" ransacked from fairy tales of yore:

A PRINCESS IS BEAUTIFUL.
A PRINCESS DRESSES FINELY.
A PRINCESS IS KIND.
A PRINCESS IS GOOD.
A PRINCESS IS OBEDIENT.

Any princess who breaks these rules will lose her tiara.

☞ But why?

To uncover the answer to this question, *Bad Princess* will take you through history and fairy tales to reveal where our fascination with princesses began. We'll look at the realities of life if you were young, female, and royal. We'll also throw in stories of those who refused to play by the rules and really *were* bad princesses. To round things out, we'll include the lives of duchesses, countesses, and other female nobles who didn't reign over a country. (In other words, no queens!)

We'll start off way back in the medieval period, when princesses really *did* live in towers, and end up in modern times, when some kick-butt royal girls are changing the rules. We'll see how our fascination with princesses may have taken root from fairy tales. And finally, we'll reveal how princesses inspired businesses such as Disney and LEGO to turn our princess obsession into big bucks. Between princess-themed films, gowns, books, dolls, tiaras, makeup kits, and accessories, princesses are *everywhere*. While these pink-hued products have encouraged the popularity of princesses as a role model for girls, others claim they've led to a "princess backlash"—a general distrust of all things feminine and sparkly. As a result, some believe princesses undermine young girls' self-esteem and independence by presenting them with an unrealistic standard of perfection, making princesses "bad" for young girls.

But are princesses in themselves *really* bad? Or were some only portrayed that way in history? Is there a way for a modern girl to reclaim this uber-feminine role model as an empowering one? Or should we just cut our losses and move on from princesses altogether? To find out, let's take a stroll through history! ♛

P IS FOR PRINCESS— AND ALSO FOR PINK

Here's the surprising truth behind the color that we most associate with princesses. Before World War II, pink was a popular color for baby boys; blue was for little girls. However, practical mamas went for all white—easier to clean in those pre-washing-machine days. More recently, the color pink has been reclaimed by women in organizations such as those that promote breast cancer awareness and the antiwar group Code Pink. Barbie® manufacturer Mattel claimed the color for its own when it chose PMS 219 pink as the trademark color for the popular doll's fiftieth anniversary in 2008. ("PMS" is an abbreviation for Pantone Matching System, a color-printing system.)

WHAT IF treason was the reason the princess was in the tower?

CHAPTER 1

A Long, Long Time Ago

> "'A princess must be polite,' she said to herself."
>
> — Frances Hodgson Burnett, *A Little Princess* (1905)

Our story begins with an overview of what legally makes a princess—and it's not about the bling.

A princess is the daughter of a king and a queen. A king and a queen are the heads of a monarchy. A monarchy is a country where the right to rule is handed down from generation to generation within a single family. In Europe, the crown is often passed on through the men in the family: The king is succeeded by his son, the prince. To keep a family's power, um, *powerful*, the law of primogeniture was applied. Primogeniture meant that a country could only pass to one male heir—no splitting lands up to give everyone a fair share. The same rules applied if you were a duke, a count, or another royal male.

Who's Who in Royalty

IN ORDER OF POWER:

EMPEROR: Wife is an empress.

KING: Wife is a queen.

PRINCE: Wife is a princess.

DUKE: Wife is a duchess.

MARQUESS: Wife is a marchioness.

EARL: Wife is a countess.

VISCOUNT: Wife is a viscountess.

BARON: Wife is a baroness.

LORD: Wife is a lady.

After reading all this, you might be thinking, "Hey, that's not fair! Why do boys get everything?" Well, it's because of a little something called Salic law.

Salic law was a judicial system that sprang up around the year 500 CE from the Frankish Empire, a group of kingdoms that by then had spread across much of continental Europe. One of Salic law's main rules stated only males could inherit land and thrones. If you were born female, tough luck.

Fortunately for girls, not all countries followed Salic law. Thanks to a technicality, Princess Alexandrina Victoria inherited the crown of Great Britain when her uncle King William IV died without a male heir in 1837. She reigned over the British Empire under the more famous name of Queen Victoria until 1901—a sixty-three-year record surpassed only in September 2015 by her great-great-granddaughter Queen Elizabeth II. And in the Netherlands, Queen Beatrix served as regent, or someone who rules over a country, for thirty-three years before abdicating, or stepping down, in 2013 to let her son have his turn.

Even so, Salic law led to wars in countries without male heirs—if there's no prince, who should rule? (In sixteenth-century England, this was a big reason why King Henry VIII married six times. He feared his country would fall into chaos if he died without a son—but we'll look into this in Chapter 3.) Yet, in a strange way, Salic law made princesses highly valuable. In the absence of a prince, someone could gain a throne by marrying a king's daughter. The film *Maleficent* depicted this situation when the decidedly unroyal Stefan wed King Henry's daughter to become king.

But what happened if there *was* a male heir? Did this mean a princess could do whatever she liked for the rest of her natural-born, pink-hued, blue-blooded life? Nope. Instead of freeing these royal girls from their responsibilities, Salic law turned princesses and other female royals into tools to be used by their families to expand territories, forge empires, and strengthen political ties.

Bottom line: Princesses had to do what they were told—and what they were told was to put a ring on it.

SOMEDAY MY PRINCE WILL COME

Royal power is a game of connections. One certain way to make connections: marriage. After all, if you're a king, the odds are good your enemy is going to play nice if he's married into your family.

THE TRUTH ABOUT ROYALTY AND BLUE BLOOD

When history describes a person as possessing "blue blood," it's shorthand for saying, "Hey, they're royal." Does this mean they actually have blue-colored blood? Of course not. Here's the strange-but-true story behind this long-established belief: If you have light-colored skin on the inside of your wrist, you might see blue veins snaking down from your palm. Does this mean your blood is blue? Nope, it's an optical illusion: The closer your veins are to the surface of your skin, the bluer they appear.

However, this simple truth didn't stop Spanish nobles from bragging about their *sangre azul*—Spanish for "blue blood"—in the ninth century. They used this expression to differentiate themselves from their Moorish enemies, whose darker-skinned wrists were less likely to reveal blue veins. From here the term "blue blood" spread across Europe, and came to mean a person of aristocratic ancestry.

In reality, some living creatures *do* have blue blood: lobsters, crabs, and other sea creatures. Last we heard, they're not claiming any thrones. Yet.

And so off to the chapel the princesses were sent for the sake of their countries. Unlike Cinderella, who got lucky with her Prince Charming, most princesses were expected to wed without complaints to whomever their family decided. (True love? Forget about it!) Often the princesses were sent far from home, never to encounter their royal parents and siblings again during their lives.

Think it was easy to nab a dreamy prince or duke? Not usually. When it came to marriage, it didn't matter if the groom was handsome, smart, or even the same age as his bride-to-be. Nor was it considered a problem if the groom was related by blood. In some cases, this was considered desirable because it helped keep power within a royal family.

A princess's life changed once she said "I do." Often marriage would turn her tiara into a crown, making her a queen, which gained her new responsibilities in her adopted country. Most important, the princess was expected to start a family with her new husband, so there would be heirs to inherit the throne. The birth of new princes and princesses meant that royal power would continue into a new generation, bringing political stability to a monarchy.

Here's one "good" princess considered a raging success by the standards of her time:

Margaret Fredkulla (c. 1080–1130) was a princess of Sweden. Her father, King Inge I, arranged for her to marry King Magnus of Norway to ensure peace between their lands. (*Fredkulla* translates as "Peace-Maiden.") After Magnus kicked the bucket two years after their wedding, Queen Margaret left Norway. This displeased her subjects, who had expected her to remain there to keep things peaceful. But Margaret had another husband in mind: King Niels of Denmark.

To his credit, Niels recognized that Margaret was smarter than he was. He encouraged her to rule Denmark in his place, giving her power over all she surveyed. If that wasn't fabulous enough, Margaret gave birth to two princes, one who survived to inherit the Danish throne after his parents' deaths.

Let's break down Princess Margaret's queenly life: arranged marriage. *Check.* Moving around from country to country. *Check.* Creating peace.

Margaret letting loose the doves of peace from the chapel of love.

Check. Ruling a kingdom. *Check.* Providing the king with heirs to his throne. *Double check.*

Was Margaret happy? Who knows? On parchment, she was praised because she did right by Denmark as its ruler. However, no matter how fancy the gowns, or respected the crown, a medieval girl toiling in the fields probably wasn't that aware of the nitty-gritty of Margaret's royal situation.

But then things shifted on the "who wants to be a princess" front. *One reason: some musicians called troubadours.*

THE TROUBADOURS: ALL SINGING, ALL TRAVELING!

Let's close our eyes and time-travel back a thousand years to the eleventh century. It's an era when girls tucked their hair beneath headdresses called wimples, and boys wore dress-like tunics instead of T-shirts. There are no electronics, no cable TV. No airplanes or Wi-Fi. Even so, some things remain the same: Music makes people happy.

Enter the troubadour. Not only did these talented musicians write and compose their own songs, they also performed them. To gain new audiences, they moved from village to village—or castle to castle—crooning tunes to appreciative crowds. Because many troubadour songs were written down, their music survives to this day. They sang in a variety of styles about everything from the adventures of the Crusades to the trials of true love. Their music even encouraged listeners to kick up their heels and dance.

A popular song subject was the *princesse lointaine*—"distant princess"—a sublimely beautiful royal lady the composer was totally crushing

Monsieur Emo Musician Dude. The Ed Sheeran of his time.

on. In most cases, the troubadour never even laid eyes on the *princesse lointaine* before penning his lovesick songs in her honor. Her reputation was enough to enflame his eternal devotion.

In a way, these songs could be viewed as the first instance of princess publicity. They served to spread the idea of what a princess should be—an exquisitely beautiful girl—in the same way *People* magazine does today for starlets.

One troubadour, Jaufre Rudel, really bought into the whole *princesse lointaine* thing. His unnamed biographer wrote that Rudel:

"... fell in love with the countess of Tripoli, without seeing her, for the praise he heard of her from the pilgrims who came from Antioch; and he composed many songs about her with remarkable melodies but less beautiful verses."

The *princesse lointaine* who inspired Rudel to write songs of "less beautiful verses" was *Hodierna of Tripoli* (c. 1110–1164), a princess of Jerusalem. The princess gained the title of countess when her father, King Baldwin II of Jerusalem, married her off to Raymond II of Tripoli. The marriage was complicated at best. Hodierna had three sisters who schemed behind the scenes with her. In addition, Raymond grew jealous that the countess liked someone else more than him—and that other men *really* liked her in return. After all, Hodierna was reputed to be beyond gorgeous.

Though princesses have been around for as long as there have been monarchies, chances are girls way back when didn't yearn to be pretty-in-pink like they do today. One possible reason: Old-time tales of princesses usually didn't end happily. Ancient Greece seemed to specialize in hard-luck princess myths. For example, Princess Danae, a princess of the Greek city of Argos, was walled up in a tower just like Rapunzel. The reason? Her father, King Acrisius, had been warned that Danae's future son would kill for Acrisius's throne. This was only the beginning of the princess's adventures. Thanks to the divine intervention of the god Zeus, who fell in love with her, Danae gave birth to a healthy boy, Perseus. Instead of sending his grandson a gift, King Daddy locked Danae and baby Perseus inside a wooden chest and threw them into the sea. Danae and Perseus survived against the odds to fulfill the prophecy—proof you can't outsmart destiny.

In another Greek myth, Princess Ariadne was abandoned on an island by her boyfriend, Theseus, after rescuing him from a labyrinth inhabited by the Minotaur—a half-man/half-bull monster. Though Dionysus, the god of wine and good times, eventually fell in love with Ariadne, the princess never recovered from Theseus's betrayal. If that wasn't bad enough, some claim that later Perseus (remember him?) killed Ariadne in battle after he became king. However, the poet Homer wrote that Artemis, goddess of the hunt, killed Ariadne with an arrow because the princess was too heartbroken to live without Theseus.

Lesson learned by the girls of ancient Greece: Princesshood leads to imprisonment, abandonment, and, worst of all, seasickness.

From here, it's easy to connect the dots: Rudel probably heard those wild stories about Hodierna's beauty. This caused him to fall hard for Her Royal Majesty. He composed songs in her honor. They included verses such as: *"Distant are the castle and tower where she lies with her husband . . . my mind is over there near her."* Some even claim he traveled to Tripoli to declare his devotion to his *princesse lointaine*, using the Crusades as his excuse.

After all this drama, did the troubadour and the princess who inspired his music live happily ever after? Did they even meet?

Rudel's biographer offers the story that they *did* meet—but as Rudel was breathing his last. You see, he'd fallen dangerously ill while traveling to the Holy Land. Though everyone thought Rudel was a goner, they brought his body to an inn and managed to collect Hodierna from her jealous husband.

In a scene like something out of *The Fault in Our Stars*, Hodierna rushed to her never-before-seen troubadour admirer:

". . . and took him in her arms, and he knew she was the Countess, and recovered consciousness, and praised God and thanked Him for having let him live to see her. And so he died in his lady's arms."

Most conclude this story is fanciful at best—but it's a good one. History states that Hodierna ruled in Raymond's stead when he was killed in battle; the crown was passed to her son, Raymond III, when he came of age.

However, in the case of *Joan, Lady of Wales and Lady of Snowdon* (1191–1237), it turned out her husband was right: She *was* a bad princess.

Joan was the out-of-wedlock daughter of King John of England; evidence suggests her mother might not have been blue-blooded. Despite Joan's uncertain status, her father deployed her as he would any princess: He arranged for her to marry Llywelyn the Great of the neighboring kingdom of North Wales.

For the first twenty-five years of their marriage, all seemed well: Joan gave birth to an heir and did all the good royal-wife stuff. But then she did something unexpected: She fell in love with William de Braose the Younger, a nobleman. When the two of them were caught kissing in the queen's chambers in 1230, their forbidden love was no longer a secret.

It wasn't pretty. The court was shocked. Llywelyn was furious. Yet his treatment of Joan was far gentler than expected—perhaps a quarter century of marriage meant something after all.

Llywelyn had Joan locked away in another part of the castle. William's fate was not nearly as kind: He was hanged to death. ♛

FROG Princess or VATICAN Princess?

CHAPTER 2

The Lucrezia Borgia Cookbook

"It is my duty to be good to my husband and make myself beautiful for him. God has shown me how to do this, so I would be unwise not to."

—Countess Elizabeth Báthory (1560–1614)

One assumption about being a princess is you can do whatever you want, like *Charlie and the Chocolate Factory's* Veruca Salt. ("Daddy! I want an Oompa-Loompa!") But, as we're already starting to see, the life of the average princess was above average when it came to restraints. Most princesses didn't have any choice but to follow their family's commands—or else. Under such circumstances, all the jewels and gowns in the world couldn't make up for a life without free will.

Despite this cold, hard truth, some royal girls did what they could to have their cake and eat it, too—or so sources claim.

In Renaissance Italy, *Lucrezia Borgia* (1480–1519), an unofficial princess of the Vatican, a nation-state inside Rome, poisoned her enemies for the sake of love and loyalty. Her alleged poison of choice: *la cantarella*, a concoction that most likely contained arsenic and cantharidin, an odorless toxin secreted by blister beetles. About fifty years after Lucrezia's death, *Countess Elizabeth Báthory* (1560–1614) earned the nickname "the Blood Countess"—but not because of her blue blood. The countess was responsible for the deaths of hundreds of girls.

Are these shocking stories true? Or were they malicious gossip spread by jealous underlings?

DINNER WITH LUCREZIA

Five hundred years ago, being pope of the Catholic Church was like being king of a powerful country. Only instead of a country, it was the Vatican (which actually is a country, though a really small one). Not only did old-school popes control unfathomable riches, they also wielded tremendous power. However, unlike a king, you didn't have to have royal blood to be

Lucrezia Borgia. Bad? Or just painted that way?

pope—but you did need to be a cardinal. (A cardinal is considered a prince of the church.) It also didn't hurt to be ambitious and cunning, especially since Italy at that time was not a united country.

Cardinal Rodrigo Borgia possessed both ambition and cunning, along with something extra: an exquisitely beautiful daughter named Lucrezia. Besides Lucrezia, Rodrigo had two sons, Cesare and Juan. They were more than willing to dirty their hands on Daddy's behalf.

If one was to believe all the stories told about the Borgias, their family motto should have been "The Family That Slays Together Stays Together." Their involvement in the church was to further their ambitions on earth rather than serve the kingdom of God. Cardinals weren't supposed to have children, but Rodrigo did—and he flaunted them in public. Cesare was especially known for his ruthlessness. When Juan's corpse was discovered in the Tiber River, it was whispered Cesare was to blame; he'd supposedly killed his brother to nab his worldly goods. As for Lucrezia, some accused her of poisoning boyfriends and enemies at dinner—another reason to avoid breaking bread with the Borgias.

Lucrezia's supposed method was like something out of a James Bond movie: She wore a hollow ring that poured *la cantarella* into an enemy's goblet of wine with a flick of her finger. The victims would never notice when the poisoning took place, for they'd be too distracted by Lucrezia's lovely face, lithe figure, and long golden hair. No one would ever expect a girl who looked like an angel to behave so cruelly.

Alas, the truth wasn't nearly as exciting as the rumors: No proof has ever been found that Lucrezia Borgia poisoned anyone. Instead, she did as she was told: She married to cement her father's power like a good princess should. And that's where things got complicated.

Here's a quick trip through the roller-coaster love life of Lucrezia Borgia, Vatican Princess:

1. When Lucrezia was ten, Rodrigo contracted her to marry Querubi de Centelles, the son of the Count of Oliva. Before they made it to the chapel, Daddy decided de Centelles wasn't good enough for his precious girl.

2. The same thing happened to Lucrezia's next engagement, which went bust two months after the first.

3. Meanwhile, in Rome, Rodrigo was upgraded from cardinal to pope and took on the title Alexander VI. This upped Lucrezia's worth as a wife big time—everybody wanted a pope in the family!

4. When Lucrezia turned thirteen, she tied the knot at last. Husband #1 was Giovanni Sforza, a dude double her age; Rodrigo chose the groom as a thank-you to the Sforzas for helping him become pope. Lucrezia had a suitably lavish wedding that would have made the cover of *Renaissance Bride* magazine, had there been one.

5. Four years later, Pope Alexander fell out with the Sforza family. He decided Husband #1 wasn't a good fit for Lucrezia and began to make (cough, cough) *plans*. Fearing for his life, Giovanni ran away. The marriage was annulled. (An annulment is a legal ruling that states a marriage never existed because of an impediment, such as fraud or family relation. An annulment is different from a divorce, where the couple decides to end a marriage, usually due to incompatibility.)

6. In 1498, Lucrezia married Husband #2, Alfonso d'Aragon, but made the mistake of falling in love with him. Less than two years after their nuptials, Alfonso was stabbed while walking home from the Vatican—turned out he had been disloyal to the Borgias. After Alfonso survived the attack, Cesare arranged for someone to kill him. Lucrezia's constant weeping while she mourned Alfonso got on Pope Alexander's nerves, so he sent her away to help her recover from her loss.

7. Two years later, Husband #3 stepped up to the altar once Lucrezia was over Husband #2. The reluctant groom was Alfonso d'Este, the future Duke of Ferrara; Lucrezia's massive dowry persuaded him to marry into the Borgias. (More about dowries on page 47.) Neither spouse was crazy about the other, but Lucrezia settled down to do what a good princess should: give birth to lots of kids. Yet she was more than just a Renaissance mom. She became a patron of the arts, invested wisely in marshland for development, and did all sorts of good deeds for the citizens of Ferrara—in other words, she was no bad princess. By the time of her death in childbirth at the age of thirty-nine, she was considered a downright outstanding member of society.

Despite all this, all anyone ever remembers of Lucrezia Borgia is that poison ring. Which, when you think about it, does sound pretty cool, in a how-bad-can-a-princess-be way.

However, even if Lucrezia did what the rumors said, her alleged crimes were nothing compared to the bone-chilling wickedness of the Countess Elizabeth Báthory.

BLOOD, BEAUTY, & BEYOND

In Slovakia, a ruined castle dating from the thirteenth century rests high on a lonely hill. The gray stone structure goes by the name Čachtice Castle, after the village located closest to it. Even if you didn't know the castle's history, it would still give you the creeps—Čachtice Castle looks like the kind of place that would house a vampire. And, in a sense, it did.

Four hundred years earlier, the castle was home to the world's most prolific serial killer, "blood countess" Elizabeth Báthory.

You'd never have believed it to look at her. Like Lucrezia, Elizabeth was lovely to behold. Her portrait reveals a young woman resembling Snow White: pale skin, ebony hair, and large mournful eyes. Based on appearance alone, it's hard to imagine her harming a fly. Elizabeth's background also suggests little cause for violence. She was raised by Hungary's richest and most powerful family. She was well educated, and could read and write in several languages. At the age of fourteen, she married a nobleman, Ferenc Nádasdy, who was an acclaimed war hero. The couple's union produced three children before Ferenc's death in 1604.

Yet one December night in 1610, Elizabeth and four of her servants were arrested for killing an unfathomable number of girls; a witness at her trial testified there were as many as 650 based on a register kept by the countess. The reason for the murders? No one really knows, though local legend claimed Elizabeth believed she could magically preserve her beauty by bathing in blood. (Talk about gross!)

It's mind-boggling to imagine how so many murders might have occurred. Where could Elizabeth have hidden all those corpses? If you were a servant at the castle, wouldn't you have gone to the authorities and said,

Countess Elizabeth Báthory. Bad to the bone.

"There's some nasty stuff going on with the countess"? Wouldn't villagers have noticed the sinister goings-on at Čachtice Castle?

The truth was, villagers *did* notice. But it took time for the authorities to take action—after all, Elizabeth ruled the land where they lived. For years there'd been whispers of disturbances at the castle: blood-curdling screams in the middle of the night, maids disappearing for no reason. Clergy observed an unnatural uptick in the deaths of girls who lived under Elizabeth's roof. When questioned, she'd claim they'd all died of cholera at the same time, or killed one another fighting over jewelry. In 1602, eight years before the countess's arrest, a minister made an official complaint after Elizabeth presented him with corpses to bury. Nothing was done. Bodies were dumped over castle walls and hidden in canals.

Despite this, girls still came to Čachtice Castle. Peasants sent their daughters to serve the countess—she paid too generously to be refused. When local victims grew scarce, the countess opened a finishing school for young female aristocrats. The poor girls never returned to their families.

Many deaths later, authorities confronted the countess—they could no longer ignore the evidence. Elizabeth's servants, who'd participated in the murders, stood trial; to avoid scandalizing the Báthory family, Elizabeth was simply imprisoned. While accounts of the trial vary, as many as three hundred witnesses are believed to have testified to the atrocities committed at Čachtice Castle. Elizabeth had previously proclaimed any allegations against her to be "mad lies" despite the overwhelming evidence.

Fairest in the Land?

If the Countess Báthory really bathed in blood to remain fairest in the land, she wasn't that different from Snow White's evil stepmother. When the queen discovered her stepdaughter outranked her in beauty, she decided to kill her—and, like the Countess Báthory, found herself in trouble. Both royal women offer extreme examples of What Can Go Wrong when vanity overtakes reason.

However, the Countess Báthory and Snow White's stepmom aren't alone in taking dangerous measures to improve on what Mother Nature gave them. Centuries of upper-class Chinese women suffered foot binding, leaving them barely able to walk. This painful practice came about because small feet (known as "lotus feet") were considered beautiful; from as early as the age of five, the bones of girls' feet were broken and bent into an unnatural shape. In Renaissance England, Elizabethan noblewomen painted their faces with ceruse, a toxic mixture of white lead and vinegar, to gain fashionably pale skin. More recently, nineteenth-century women swallowed poisonous arsenic pills to improve their complexions; accidental overdoses were not uncommon. Tightly laced corsets could give Victorian ladies malformed organs and broken ribs.

While it's easy to look back and judge our ancestors, people really aren't that different now. Instead of lead-based creams, some use cosmetics to enhance their faces. Instead of foot binding, others undergo painful plastic surgery. Alas, the more things change, the more they remain the same: It seems we'll still do anything to remain fairest in the land.

As punishment, Elizabeth's servants were immediately executed in a horribly gory fashion. But the Blood Countess got off easy because of her noble blood. She was walled up for the rest of her life in her castle chamber without Internet—and hopefully without a mirror. ♛

Mirror, mirror on the wall,

Many beliefs about princesses were stoked by fairy tales, such as "Cinderella" and "Snow White." Though girls usually discover Cindy & Co. from books and movies, the first fairy tales arose from stories told through the oral tradition. "Oral tradition" refers to stories passed down from one generation to the next through the spoken word. Sometimes these words were even sung, like a troubadour's ballad.

In an age without television, movies, or books, storytelling was the only way to go. Beyond this, elements of fairy tales can be tracked all the way back to Greek and Roman mythology. Remember the story of Princess Ariadne and the Minotaur? Here's another example of a long-ago princess myth resembling a fairy tale: The Roman story of Cupid and Psyche is about a beautiful girl imprisoned in a palace by a monster who's really a good guy in disguise. Sounds kind of like the plot of "Beauty and the Beast," doesn't it?

While many of these stories survived oral tradition to be written down, it wasn't until 1550 that the first European fairy tales were published in a book. *Le piacevoli notti* (*The Pleasant Nights*) was a collection of seventy-four stories, of which only fifteen were fairy tales. (You gotta start somewhere.) It was authored by Giovanni Francesco Straparola; little is known about him beyond that he lived in Venice. Straparola presented his stories as originating from the make-believe court of Princess Lucretia (no relation to Vatican princess Lucrezia Borgia).

How widely read was *Le piacevoli notti*? Was it popular enough to set fire to the princess dreams of sixteenth-century girls? Probably not—books were expensive and rare back then. Regardless, *Le piacevoli notti* influenced the fairy tales of the better-known Brothers Grimm and Charles Perrault to come.

Too many PRINCESSES. Too many DOWRIES.

CHAPTER 3:

Princess Wars

> "*I could sooner reconcile all Europe than two women.*"
>
> — Louis XIV of France (1638–1715)

hile Lucrezia was obeying Daddy Pope for the good of the Borgias, and Elizabeth was bathing in blood for the good of her beauty, things were different up north. And it wasn't just the climate.

In Renaissance England, two branches of the royal family battled to grab control of the country in a decades-long war that at times resembled toddlers squabbling over a Happy Meal toy. ("My throne!" "No, *mine!*") The ongoing struggle became known as the War of the Roses. A legend claims this is because one family branch, the House of York, identified itself with a white rose; the second, the House of Lancaster, with a red rose.

The War of the Roses was finally settled in 1485 at the Battle of Bosworth Field. The winner? Henry Tudor from the House of Lancaster, who ruled England as King Henry VII. To soften the blow to the losing house, he married Elizabeth of York, uniting the Lancaster and York branches into the new-and-improved House of Tudor. Henry VII was the first of the Tudor monarchs; his son Henry VIII succeeded him in 1509. Because of all the trouble the Tudors went through to win the throne, Henry VIII became obsessed with making sure his family didn't lose it.

A hundred and forty-three years later on the other side of the English Channel in France, a four-year-old boy named Louis got a throne of his own in a more peaceful fashion: His father died. Under the title King Louis XIV, he would reign for a jaw-dropping seventy-two years, earning the nickname "the Sun King" in the process.

Though over a century and a body of water separated their reigns, Tudor King Henry and Sun King Louis had one problem in common: their princess daughters.

MY KINGDOM FOR A SON

Imagine that you're a princess from way back when. Your father, the king, cherishes you and your queen mother, whom he married out of love and duty. Despite you being an only child—and a girl at that—life is okay. Your dad respects your mom enough to involve her in the ruling of your country. He's nice to you, though he never stops obsessing about wanting a son to wear the family crown. You figure that if push comes to shove, Dad will find a way to give you the crown—he's smart like that. Maybe he'll even marry you to that dude from Spain you've been crushing on so you can rule together.

Just another day at the court of Henry VIII.

One day when you're a teenager, King Daddy comes home with big news. He announces he was never *really* married to your mother because she'd been previously married to someone else in the family. This means you're no longer a princess. Oh, and by the way, he's already picked out a stepmom for you, and she's pregnant with a baby that he bets will be a son.

This was the story of Princess Mary (1516–1558), the eldest daughter of Tudor king Henry VIII. Mary's mom was Henry's first queen, Catherine of Aragon, whom he divorced to wed Anne Boleyn, the daughter of a courtier. (A courtier is someone who's a member of a royal court.) As for Anne, she gave birth to Henry's second daughter, Princess Elizabeth (1533–1603), a mere three months after Henry crowned her queen.

But it was Queen Catherine who had the last laugh: Anne was only Wife #2 in Henry's scandalous love life. He went on to marry a total of six times.

Here's how it went down in Tudor Town.

Daddy Dearest

DEADLIEST

→ A TIMELINE ←

> If at first you don't succeed, wed, wed again.

Princesses Elizabeth and Mary's father married six times during his reign as a result of his quest for a male heir. Only two of his wives survived the experience. Read on to find out who!

Henry VIII

WIFE

№ 1

Catherine of Aragon

(aka Mary's mum)

MARRIED 1509 *to* 1536

Henry's first bride was his brother Arthur's widow. After more than two decades of marriage, one daughter, and no living sons later, he decided the marriage was illegal—he was wrong to marry his sister-in-law. **RESULT: Divorce; death in exile**

Anne Boleyn was the real reason Henry dumped Catherine. The king decided Anne had the right stuff to give him his much-desired son. When she didn't, accusations of treason and adultery were trumped up. **RESULT: Beheaded**

WIFE

№ 2

Anne Boleyn

(aka Elizabeth's mum)

MARRIED 1533 *to* 1536

WIFE No. 3

Jane Seymour

Third time was the charm: Edward, Henry's only male heir, was born to Jane soon after they said "I do." Alas, the king's rejoicing was cut short when the queen's health worsened after the birth. **RESULT: Death**

MARRIED 1536 to 1537

Henry's fourth marriage was arranged by his right-hand man, Thomas Cromwell. The king didn't meet his bride until it was time to wed. It was not love at first sight. **RESULT: Annulment for Anne; beheading for Cromwell**

WIFE No. 4

Anne of Cleves

MARRIED 1540 to 1540

Catherine Howard

WIFE No. 5

Catherine was a fun-loving teenager when the more-than-double-her-age Henry decided she was the bee's knees. After getting caught kissing another, Catherine's reign was wrung. **RESULT: Beheaded**

MARRIED 1540 to 1542

WIFE No. 6

Henry's last adventure in matrimony was to a twice-married childless widow. Loyal Catherine was rumored to have nursed the king in his final illness. **RESULT: Survived**

Catherine Parr

WINNER!

MARRIED 1543 to 1547

After two wives, one beheading, and a whole lot of drama, Henry was lucky to have Wife #3, Jane Seymour, who gave birth to a living son, Edward. Henry was pumped. Now that there was a boy in the house, nobody could steal the English throne from the Tudors.

As for Mary and Elizabeth, after Henry divorced Mary's mother and beheaded Elizabeth's, he declared neither of them to be real princesses. If that wasn't bad enough, they were stuck dealing with stepmother after stepmother after stepmother.

Some of the princesses' stepmothers were great: Wife #3, Jane Seymour, healed rifts between Henry and his daughters. Others . . . not so much: Wife #2, Anne Boleyn, delighted in plotting mayhem to undermine Mary. The sisters finally got lucky with Wife #6, Catherine Parr. She convinced Henry to restore both Mary and Elizabeth to the line of succession whether or not they were princesses. This meant Edward got first dibs on the throne, Mary second, and Elizabeth last-but-not-least.

However, unlike today's blended families, the stakes were much higher for Mary and Elizabeth. One false step and they'd be locked up—or worse, beheaded. If that wasn't enough, some said Mary and Elizabeth shouldn't rule England in spite of Henry's decision about the line of succession. This made the sisters feel as secure as an unlocked bank vault.

When princesses feel powerless, they're forced to scheme to survive—and that's exactly what happened with Mary and Elizabeth Tudor. Though both women eventually became queen of

England, they never forgot how it felt to dance in and out of Daddy's favor during his six marriages.

MARY VS. ELIZABETH: THE WAR OF A LIFETIME

In some ways, the saga of Henry VIII and his princesses reveals the dark side of kingly entitlement: *Tired of your queen? Get a new one!* In time, Henry's actions would affect all of Europe, though at first it seemed he'd successfully preserved England for the Tudor dynasty.

Upon Henry's death in 1547, Edward became king. But here's the deal: Edward hadn't married before he became deathly ill with what may have been tuberculosis, a bacterial disease that attacks the lungs. It seemed certain the throne would pass to his sister Mary since no wife = no heirs. But that's not what happened. Before King Edward VI kicked the bucket in 1553 at the tender age of sixteen, courtiers managed to put Lady Jane Grey, Henry's teenaged great-niece, on the throne instead.

Mary rallied an army. She even got Elizabeth to go along with her plan when Mary claimed her crown.

After a reign of only nine days, Queen Jane was shoved off the throne by the new Queen Mary I. Later, Jane lost her head for treason. Now paranoid (who can blame her?), Mary hunkered down to consolidate her power. She imprisoned Elizabeth in the Tower of London (so much for sisterly affection!) and wed Philip II of Spain with the aim of giving birth to an heir. Finally, Parliament decided Philip should rule in Mary's stead if the queen died in childbirth and until their kid was old enough, pushing Elizabeth further from the throne.

Soon things *really* turned into a soap opera. Once Mary believed she was pregnant, she moved Elizabeth to court to keep tabs on her. But the pregnancy was a false alarm. Then King Philip nagged Elizabeth to marry his cousin Emmanuel Philibert, Duke of Savoy, to keep the crown in the family, in case Mary remained childless. (Savoy was a region near the borders of Germany and Italy.) Elizabeth refused.

When Mary proved unable to have kids, she had no choice but to grudgingly restore Elizabeth to the line of succession—and not a moment too soon. Queen Mary I died at the age of forty-two after suffering unexplained fevers, headaches, and vision loss.

Princesses Mary and Elizabeth. My kingdom for a sister.

Queen Elizabeth I reigned brilliantly for the next forty-four years, leading to an era of glory and prosperity for England. Reluctant to let go of the English throne, King Philip tried to convince the new queen to marry him. (Hey, he was good enough for her sister!) But Elizabeth had learned a thing or two from the life and death of her poor headless mother, Anne Boleyn. She declared that she would rather be a beggar and single than a queen and married. When Elizabeth died at the relatively advanced age of sixty-nine, an entire nation mourned their beloved queen. However, no husband = no heirs. As a result, the Tudors lost the English throne for good, thus bringing an end to their tumultuous rule. Her father, Henry, must have turned in his grave.

In death, Mary and Elizabeth were forced to make peace. The sisters were laid to rest together in Westminster Abbey. Their shared tomb is inscribed: *Consorts in realm and tomb, here we sleep, Elizabeth and Mary, sisters, in hope of resurrection.*

BLOOD ON THE SUN

A century later, Sun King Louis XIV had his own version of Princess Wars going down in France, though the stakes were considerably lower than they'd been for Mary and Elizabeth.

The court of Louis XIV was very different from the court of Henry VIII. For starters, Louis was way less desperate than Henry had been to hold onto his throne—his queen, Marie-Thérèse, had given birth to a son a year after their wedding. Perhaps since he was secure in his dynasty, Louis spent more time having fun than obsessing about male offspring.

He expanded a hunting lodge located in Versailles, outside Paris, into the grandest, most glittery palace you could imagine. Louis loved the arts and prided himself on his ballet dancing. In several performances, he danced the role of Apollo, the Greek god associated with the sun. (Get it? Sun god—Sun King.)

Like the god Apollo, Louis viewed himself as a brilliant sun shining affection on the ladies of Versailles. Surprise, surprise: The ever-so-popular king produced at least nine children with women *outside* his marriage. While this didn't make his queen very happy, at least he wasn't like Henry VIII, who would behead a wife when love soured.

Louis at his most regal.

Let's leap forward from 1550 Italy, when the first European fairy tales were published, to the seventeenth- and eighteenth-century France of Louis XIV and his successor, Louis XV. It was then that the gilded drawing rooms of the aristocrats provided the perfect place for *Les Précieuses*—"the precious ones"—to refine their storytelling skills. *Les Précieuses* were a group of scholarly ladies who prided themselves on their refined wit and wordplay. They spent hours discussing politics, philosophy, art, and other heady matters. The ladies were especially fond of fairy tales, which they'd learned from oral tradition, and tried to outshine one another by recounting elaborate variations. Sometimes they'd even hide court gossip in their stories, a seventeenth-century version of throwing shade.

Several *Précieuses* went on to publish their stories, spurring a fascination with all things fairy. These authors include Gabrielle-Suzanne Barbot de Villeneuve (c.1695–1755) and Marie-Catherine d'Aulnoy (c.1651–1705), who was the first person to coin the expression *conte de fées*—"fairy tale." One well-known tale by de Villeneuve is "Beauty and the Beast."

Among those inspired by *Les Précieuses*: Charles Perrault (1628–1703), who retold a number of their stories, including the version of "Cinderella" that inspired the Disney classic.

Of King Louis's many girlfriends, his longest-lasting relationship was with Françoise-Athénaïs, marquise de Montespan, known as Athénaïs. The marquise was beyond gorgeous, with long glamorous curls and sparkling blue eyes. She was also very witty. A contemporary said Athénaïs possessed "a beautiful mouth and fine teeth, but her expression was always insolent. . . . She had beautiful blonde hair and lovely hands and arms." The king was smitten. He rewarded her with riches and palaces beyond compare. She, in turn, gave birth to seven children by him.

Here's an overview of Louis and his complicated family.

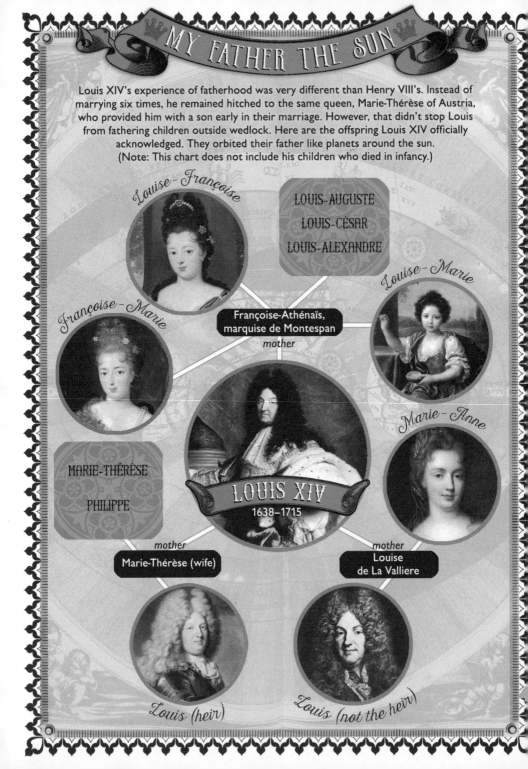

MY FATHER THE SUN

Louis XIV's experience of fatherhood was very different than Henry VIII's. Instead of marrying six times, he remained hitched to the same queen, Marie-Thérèse of Austria, who provided him with a son early in their marriage. However, that didn't stop Louis from fathering children outside wedlock. Here are the offspring Louis XIV officially acknowledged. They orbited their father like planets around the sun.
(Note: This chart does not include his children who died in infancy.)

Louise-Françoise

LOUIS-AUGUSTE
LOUIS-CÉSAR
LOUIS-ALEXANDRE

Louise-Marie

Françoise-Marie

Françoise-Athénaïs,
marquise de Montespan
mother

MARIE-THÉRÈSE

PHILIPPE

Marie-Anne

LOUIS XIV
1638–1715

mother
Marie-Thérèse (wife)

mother
Louise
de La Valliere

Louis (heir)

Louis (not the heir)

You might wonder what happened to Louis's "illegitimate" daughters. Were these girls any less royal because their parents weren't married? Nope. Ever the problem-solver, Louis tried to make everyone happy by granting these daughters the title of *princesses du sang*—"princesses of the blood"—confirming their blue blood and setting them up for the good life at court. He explained, "I thought it was only just to assure this child of the honor of her birth."

However, like Henry VIII's daughters, two of Louis's *princesses du sang* squabbled because of Daddy Dearest. Instead of a throne, they fought over dowries. Both were daughters of Athénaïs, so you'd think these sisters could get along. Spoiler alert: They didn't.

Louis gave *Louise-Françoise de Bourbon, Princess of Condé* (1673–1743), a dowry of one million livres—the French currency at the time—when he ordered her to marry a distantly related cousin, Louis, Duc de Bourbon-Condé. Though Louise-Françoise was two months short of turning twelve, she was already exquisitely beautiful, like her mother. She was also old enough to understand her groom was not a handsome Prince Charming. Nor was he very nice: He seemed to think everyone should go around Versailles kissing up to him because of his royal position.

Louise-Françoise did her best to distract herself from the unwanted marriage. She gambled to the point of debt and got a cute boyfriend on the side. But then her younger sister *Françoise-Marie de Bourbon, Duchess of Orleans* (1677–1749), was married off by King Louis. The groom? Philippe, Duc de Chartres, who ranked higher than Louise-Françoise's unpleasant snob of a husband. Françoise-Marie reportedly said of the match, "I don't care if he loves me, so long as he marries me."

Louise-Françoise was beyond peeved, for she would have to bow down to her baby sister for the rest of her life. But that wasn't the worst of it. Turned out Papa had given Françoise-Marie *double* the dowry for her wedding—a tactless move on the Sun King's part. Talk about rubbing salt in a wound!

From then on, the sisters viewed each other as bitter rivals. Lesson learned by Louis: Treat all your princesses equally when it comes to gift-giving—or husband-giving. 👑

Louis's princesses *du sang* before they were at each other's throats.

Dowries:
The Ultimate Wedding Gift

Remember our old friend Salic law, which let boys inherit thrones and turned girls into pawns on the royal-marriage market? Here's another reason folks wanted a princess bride: They came bearing a dowry—wealth bestowed from the bride's family estate.

Though it's tempting to think of dowries as Salic law's consolation prize for being born female, dowries are very different from inheritances. For starters, dowries aren't bestowed at death, only at marriage. Dowries also predate Salic law: The Code of Hammurabi, a system of laws from ancient Mesopotamia, states that the dowry remained property of the bride and could only be inherited by her children from the marriage. However, in ancient Rome, the dowry was transferred directly to the husband's family. Whatever the culture, the main purpose of the dowry was to ensure girls went into their marriage with some financial security. They also helped set up the newly married couple's household. Dowries still exist today in some cultures and countries.

While a dowry could be comprised of money, as in the case of Louis XIV's feuding daughters, it could also include property: land, housing, jewels, linens, and domesticated animals. (Herd of cows, anyone?) A generous dowry could even help make a less-than-fetching bride more appealing to suitors. Sounds harsh, right? But remember, marriage then wasn't about love; it was about the consolidation of power and property.

The French Revolution was a real BEAST.

CHAPTER 4:

Those Revolting Royals

> "They are dying of jealousy, for I am a princess, a real princess."
>
> —Pauline Bonaparte

In the eighteenth century, the age of absolute rule by kings like Henry VIII and Louis XIV turned into something toxic if you were royal: revolution.

On July 4, 1776, the American colonies affirmed their right to pursue life, liberty, and happiness by signing the Declaration of Independence; they'd already taken up muskets against England's King George III. After years of paying high taxes to their imperial overlords, the colonists had had enough. Their war for independence was aided by French allies, who had never liked the Brits that much anyway.

The result? Good-bye, monarchy; hello, democracy!

Just over a decade later, France followed America's example by shaking off their royal shackles at home. Ironically, one cause of the French Revolution was governmental debt from helping America. But even before then, France had experienced years of scanty harvests, leaving the poor without bread and resentful of the aristocracy. The French Revolution was capped by the beheading of King Louis XVI and Queen Marie Antoinette in 1793.

The result? Good-bye, monarchy; hello, Reign of Terror!

The Reign of Terror was born of the chaos after the revolution. Though it lasted just under a year, it was marked by the executions of 40,000 accused "enemies of the revolution." Its main aim was to wipe out anyone with a drop of royal blood, but non-aristocrats were also marched to the guillotine. All it took to lose your head was to be in the wrong place at the wrong time.

Bottom line: It was no longer cool to be a princess. However, even before the Reign of Terror rumbled into town, the winds had shifted—a lesson learned the hard way by the *Princesse de Lamballe* (1749–1792).

TO THE BITTER END

The Princesse de Lamballe was a devoted friend to Queen Marie Antoinette long before the French Revolution tore the country apart. This princess had been royal *before* her marriage. She'd been born Princess Marie-Thérèse Louise of Savoy-Carignan. (Savoy was a region near the borders of Germany and Italy.) Her hubby, Louis Alexandre, the

Prince de Lamballe, was a great-grandson of Louis XIV and a wild party animal. In contrast, the Princesse de Lamballe was famed for her pure morals and gentle heart, which had won her the nickname "the Good Angel."

When Louis Alexandre dropped dead from too much partying a year after marrying the princess, Marie Antoinette swooped in to make his twenty-year-old widow her BFF. The queen sweetened the deal by appointing the Princesse de Lamballe as her Superintendent of the Household, a position that paid 150,000 livres a year. At a time when peasants were starving, this wasn't the smartest move for a queen nicknamed Madame Deficit because of her extravagant ways.

The affection between Marie Antoinette and the princess led to cruel gossip beyond the palace walls. Offensive pamphlets and cartoons depicting the two friends as more than "just friends" were circulated all over Paris. Regardless, the Princesse de Lamballe remained loyal to Marie Antoinette when things went downhill in the revolution department. She even traveled to England to plead for help for the royal family. Afterward, the princess returned to France to stand by the queen as a patriotic act. She brought Marie Antoinette the gift of a cute spaniel to cheer her up, though she believed they were doomed.

She was right: A year after her return, the Princesse de Lamballe was imprisoned for treason. During Marie Antoinette's trial, she refused to betray the queen. The princess testified, "I have nothing to reply, dying a little earlier or later is a matter of indifference to me. I am prepared to make the sacrifice of my life."

The aristocratic world that gave birth to *Les Précieuses* and their refined *conte de fées* shuddered to a close with the French Revolution. Soon the Brothers Grimm filled the void with their first book, *Children's and Household Tales*, in 1812. These fairy tales were collected through oral tradition by the brothers, who went around Germany asking everyone's grandma for a bedtime story. Despite the G-rated title, the tales were—wait for it—*grim*: In the Grimm versions, Cinderella's stepsisters' eyes were plucked out by doves, and Snow White's evil stepmother danced herself to death while wearing red-hot shoes. Thirteen years later, the brothers published an edited version slightly more suitable for children.

Danish author Hans Christian Andersen followed suit in 1835 by publishing the first volumes of *Eventyr*—Danish for "Fantastic Tales." Unlike the Brothers Grimm, who based their stories on oral tradition, Andersen drew his fairy tales from his imagination; they included "The Little Mermaid" and "The Snow Queen," which inspired the Disney film *Frozen*. Andersen's stories catapulted into popularity once they were translated into other languages. So, long before Elsa was imploring girls to "Let It Go," Andersen's stories were inspiring princess fantasies around the world.

The verdict was swift, the punishment harsh. The Princesse de Lamballe was hacked to death by a mob. Afterward, her murderers mounted her severed head on a pole, which was paraded before the queen's window in Paris— but only after they had the princess's pretty blond hair curled and powdered by a barber. Their reason? They wanted to make sure Marie Antoinette would recognize her friend.

The Princesse de Lamballe. A most loyal princess.

THE TROUBLE WITH SISTERS

You'd think the horrific fate of the Princesse de Lamballe would be enough to put anyone off princesshood for good. Not so for *Pauline Bonaparte* (1780–1825), who, by the end of her life, had gained the right to call herself a princess *and* a duchess. Not bad for a girl born into a regular old family.

Pauline was the sister of Napoleon Bonaparte, the general who swept into power after the French Revolution. To avoid more bloodshed, things *had* to settle down—and fast. Napoleon stepped in after winning military victories on France's behalf. Once a new government was in place in 1799, Napoleon became First Consul, or head of the government. Later, he let the senate convince him to become emperor of the French Empire, a hereditary title that would be passed to his descendants. (So much for democracy!)

But even before her brother was an emperor, Pauline was the It Girl of her generation. By the time she'd turned sixteen, word of her over-the-top beauty had spread all the way to Paris from Marseilles, where the Bonapartes were living at that time. Alexandre Dumas, author of *The Three Musketeers*, described Pauline as "a charming creature . . . a petite and graceful being who wore little embroidered slippers, such as Cinderella's fairy godmother might have given her."

But as we already know, appearances can be deceiving.

Pauline might have been the Kendall Jenner of her day. But she was vain, greedy, and catty to other women. She was absurdly proud of what she proclaimed were her "natural advantages" of dainty feet and hands, dark hair and eyes, and alabaster-white skin. To preserve her pale complexion, a story claims she forced a host to knock a hole through his ceiling so a servant could shower her from above with milk. She also spent absurd amounts on clothes and jewels; for one party, she dressed as a Greek nymph and adorned her hair with grapes and bands of panther skin. She horrified polite society by modeling for a nude sculpture of Venus, the Roman goddess of love. When people expressed shock over her willingness to pose unclothed, she said, "Oh, there was a good fire in the room, so I did not take cold."

It's easy to blame Pauline's bad behavior on her brother—once

"Hey, I thought you liked art."

Napoleon became emperor, who was going to tell her *non*? However, even when she was a girl, Pauline was already a piece of work. By the age of fifteen, she had gotten romantically involved with a forty-one-year-old dude with kids and a pregnant girlfriend—but he was only the first of Pauline's boyfriends. Damage control led her family to marry her off to Napoleon's second-in-command, Victor Emmanuel Leclerc, who was a more age-appropriate twenty-five.

A year after their wedding, her son, Dermide, was born. The difficult delivery permanently affected Pauline's health; for the rest of her life, she insisted on being carried around when the pain was too much for her to walk, though this didn't stop her from betraying Leclerc with countless men. A close friend of Leclerc described Pauline as a "singular mix of all that was most complete in physical perfection, and most bizarre in moral qualities."

It didn't matter much, as the marriage was not to last. Napoleon sent the couple overseas to Saint-Domingue, a Caribbean sugar colony where there'd been slave uprisings, illness, and other dangers. Leclerc hoped to make his fortune colonizing the island for France. Instead, he wound up dead from yellow fever.

Pauline returned to France accompanied by her young son and Leclerc's coffin. Ever the opportunist, Napoleon considered ways to use the widowed-but-still-gorgeous Pauline to strengthen ties with Italy. Pauline was also getting tired of wearing black in mourning for Leclerc, though it's reported she looked fabulous in it.

As if on cue, the solution arrived in the form of an eligible prince.

Prince Camillo Borghese's illustrious ancestors included a pope. His family owned a villa in Rome, lands in Tuscany, a palazzo (palace) in Florence, and a famed collection of art and jewels. He was handsome and well dressed. He was also an uneducated fool; a contemporary described Camillo as having "nothing to say, although a lively way of saying it."

The couple fell hard for each other as soon as they met. Soon they were seen all over Paris. They eloped before Pauline's year of mourning for her first husband was complete, causing yet another scandal.

Surprise, surprise: Once Princess Pauline gained the jewels and palaces, her love for Camillo was history. The couple was at each other's throats, especially after the prince insisted Pauline's young son, Dermide, not accompany them on a trip to her favorite spa resort. Then tragedy struck: The poor boy died of a fever while separated from his mother. Once Pauline learned the worst, she cried to Camillo, "Leave, monsieur, I cannot bear the sight of you. You, the butcher of my son!"

Camillo didn't leave, and Pauline didn't forgive. Nor did she forget. After Napoleon became emperor in 1804, he elevated his family as royalty, making Pauline and Camillo princess and prince twice over. Pauline dubbed her husband "His Serene Idiot."

To appease her, Napoleon granted Pauline the title Duchess of Guastalla. Guastalla was an Italian principality of about four square miles that he'd claimed for France. Napoleon described it to his sister as "a village, a borough." Pauline was insulted—she wanted more than a dinky outpost to rule. To her credit, she was smart enough to sell Guastalla back to the Italians for a tidy profit while keeping the title for herself.

Still, when push came to shove, the princess-duchess had her brother's back, just as the Princesse de Lamballe had Marie Antoinette's.

Once Napoleon was thrown off his throne in 1814, it was Pauline who followed him into exile at Elba, an island off the coast of Italy—the only member of the Bonaparte family to do so. She explained, "I have not always loved the Emperor as I should, but as my brother he has a claim on my allegiance." When Napoleon plotted a return to power, it was Pauline who gave him the famed Borghese diamonds to fund his last disastrous military campaign. Yet she had the wisdom to observe, "I think my brother might have done better to remain First Consul." She understood that by becoming emperor, Napoleon had abandoned the democratic ideals that had won him acclaim in the first place.

In time, Pauline's wild ways were subdued by the ravages of cancer, though her vanity never left. One of her last acts before her death at forty-four was to check her appearance in a mirror. Hopefully, she approved of the view.

Nineteenth-century France wasn't the only country with shopaholic princesses. Across the Channel in England, *Georgiana, Duchess of Devonshire* (1757–1806), shared this distinction with Pauline Bonaparte, along with a reputation for being the prettiest girl for miles around. But this duchess wanted more from life than fancy gowns and a title.

Georgiana entered into an advantageous marriage to William Cavendish, the Duke of Devonshire, yearning for true love; she was only seventeen, the duke nine years older. She wrote her mother: "I have been so happy in marrying a Man I so sincerely lov'd, and experience Dayly [sic] so much of his goodness to me." Georgiana was quickly disillusioned: Three days after their splashy society wedding, her husband ignored his bride to go out on the town with his drinking buddies.

Miserable in her marriage, Georgiana put her energies into dressing for success. After being hailed as the most stylish woman of her era left her eager for new challenges, Georgiana spent her time dabbling in politics and gambling. She also had an affair with a politician, which led to her having a child out of wedlock.

Even with a politician boyfriend, there was only so much she could do to influence current affairs—remember, this was well over a century before women gained the right to vote. Gambling, however, was another matter. Day or night, the gaming table was always there.

Regrettably, Georgiana's love for gambling was greater than her skill.

The Duchess of Devonshire. A gambling beauty.

A Royal Fake

Pauline had Napoleon to marry her off to a prince. Cinderella had a fairy godmother to supply her with glass slippers. What could girls who wanted to be a princess but didn't have anyone to help them do? Why, fake it until they make it! Here are a few women who did just that.

Olivia Serres (1772–1834) and Lavinia Jannetta Horton Ryves (1797–1871) were a scheming mother-and-daughter team. Olivia claimed to be the daughter of a younger brother of King George III, and bore enough resemblance to the prince that some were convinced. She went by the title Princess Olive of Cumberland. Even after Olivia was exposed as a fraud, daughter Lavinia refused to give up the good fight—she even wrote a pamphlet begging Queen Victoria to acknowledge her as one of the family.

In Sweden, Helga de la Brache (1817–1884) presented herself as the secret daughter of King Gustav IV and Queen Frederica of Baden. A newspaper story brought her true identity to light: Princess Helga was really Aurora Florentina Magnusson, nothing more than a con artist.

Princess Caraboo was kinda cuckoo.

In 1817, a charming young woman was discovered wandering the English countryside, babbling in a mysterious language. When questioned, she claimed to be **Princess Caraboo** (1791–1864) and said she'd been abducted from her faraway island home. After much press coverage, you can guess the rest: Princess Caraboo's true name was revealed to be Mary Baker, the daughter of a Devonshire cobbler.

Perhaps the most compelling royal impostor was Anna Anderson (1896–1984), who insisted she was the Grand Duchess Anastasia Romanov, daughter of Tsar Nicholas II and Tsarina Alexandra. The real Anastasia and her family were executed in 1918 after the tsar abdicated the throne during the Russian Revolution. Here's how the mystery of Anna Anderson was finally solved:

1. In 1991, five skeletons believed to be all but two of the Russian royal family were unearthed near where the Romanovs had been executed. A DNA sample was extracted from a skeleton bone believed to belong to Tsarina Alexandra.

2. Once the DNA sample was confirmed, it was compared against DNA taken from Anna Anderson's intestine and hair. (Though Anderson died in 1984, medical samples had been preserved.) No genetic match was found.

3. If this wasn't enough to disprove Anna's claim, the final two Romanov skeletons were located in 2007, and the new discovery proved that the 1991 remains did, in fact, include Anastasia's.

Case closed!

The duchess lost huge sums of money, which brought her dangerously close to bankruptcy multiple times.

* * *

The lives of Pauline, Georgiana, and the Princess Lamballe show the problem with being a princess: Fancy jewels and great clothes don't matter if you can't control your destiny. Turn the page to see a few ways a princess's life could go south in a stolen carriage. 👑

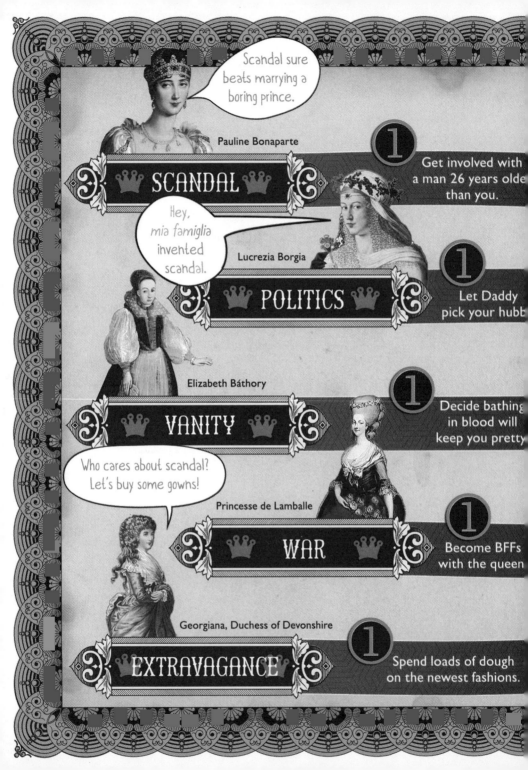

The ROYAL
ROAD TO RUIN

WHAT WE'VE LEARNED SO FAR:

Here are some of the ways a royal girl's life could crash and burn.

2 Throw shade at women not as pretty as you.

3 Pose nude for a statue that'll be displayed in public.

2 Let Daddy pick your hubby again. And again.

3 Expire after giving birth to your umpteenth child.

2 Murder a gazillion girls for their blood.

3 End up walled up in your castle forever.

2 Hang with the queen during the revolution.

3 Get beheaded by angry mob.

3 Rack up tons of debt.

2 Take up gambling in your spare time.

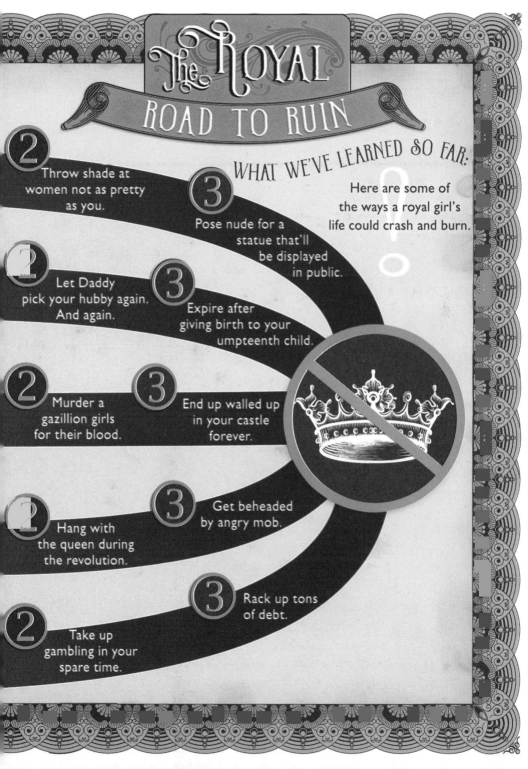

MONEY doesn't grow on trees.

CHAPTER 5:

America's Dollar Princesses

> *"The very rich are the royal families of America."*
>
> —*Town Topics* magazine, c. 1895

he Prince of Wales has entered New York."

In October 1860, these eight words opened a *New York Times* article about the visit of Albert Edward, the eldest son of Great Britain's Queen Victoria. Over 300,000 people—nearly half the population of New York City—lined Broadway to cheer the Prince of Wales's procession. Later that evening, five thousand society members crammed into an Academy of Music ballroom designed to hold only four thousand. Their combined weight caused a platform to collapse, delaying the prince's entrance until midnight. Once the ball was under way, ladies preened like Cinderellas in their best gowns and jewels to gain his attention. One reporter wrote: "Never has the Opera House presented a spectacle so sumptuous at once and so exquisite as at the moment of the Prince's entrance upon the stage, to the persuasive strains of 'God Save the Queen.'"

The roaring success of Albert's visit to the United States marked the start of America's fascination with All Things Royal over a century and a half before *Downton Abbey* aired on PBS. What had happened between the Declaration of Independence of 1776 and the prince's visit in 1860 to make New Yorkers so eager to brush shoulders with their former royal rulers?

To answer this question, let's take a look at the history of New York society.

FOUR HUNDRED REASONS TO MARRY A ROYAL

By the mid-nineteenth century, the upper class was the nearest thing Americans had to aristocracy. In New York, the upper class was made up of a group of families informally known as the Knickerbockers, who were descendants of the original Dutch settlers who had arrived in Manhattan in the seventeenth century. (The term "Knickerbocker" originated from a character's name in an 1809 book by Washington Irving about the history of New York.) But times were changing: The Industrial Revolution made it possible for ambitious Johnny-come-latelies to set themselves up in Fifth Avenue mansions despite their humble backgrounds. These upwardly mobile plutocrats—a word that means someone who earned his or her fortune through business rather than by inheritance—pounded on the doors of the Knickerbockers, eager to be one of them.

The Knickerbockers viewed these rich upstarts as hopelessly vulgar but as impossible to ignore as a Kardashian's Instagram feed. The Knickerbockers wrung their hands as they fretted what to do.

The solution came from Mrs. Caroline Astor, who'd been born a Knickerbocker but married into the family that had produced America's first multimillionaire. Inspired by a suggestion from fellow Knickerbocker Ward McAllister, Mrs. Astor built a ballroom designed to accommodate only four hundred guests drawn from the most elite families.

This exclusive list became known as the Four Hundred.

When it came to the Four Hundred, either you were *in*, or you were *out*. Guess who was out? The plutocrats. Guess who couldn't find suitable husbands for their unmarried daughters? Again: the plutocrats. But they wouldn't give up so easily. To get around Mrs. Astor's ironclad list, they cast their eyes overseas. If New York's Four Hundred wouldn't acknowledge their daughters, Paris and London would.

Between 1860 and 1914, nearly five hundred American heiresses crossed the Atlantic Ocean to wed royals in England and other European countries, creating what newspapers called "Dollar Princesses." These brides took as much as $220,000,000 in their luggage in 1911 dollars,

How to Wed a Prince

(or Lord or Duke or Earl or Viscount)

Why, yes, I am a duke!

STEP ONE:

As the daughter of an American plutocrat, your childhood is filled with lessons: music and art, French and other languages, and more. There are even riding lessons so you'll know what to do when it's time to go fox hunting. If that's not enough, you'll also attend finishing school, where you'll learn to dance a quadrille and flutter a fan.

The Eiffel Tower was opened to the public in 1889—another reason for Americans to love Paris.

STEP TWO:

Once you turn eighteen or so, you'll sail across the Atlantic to get cultured in the European way. Practice your languages with native speakers, view great art, and smooth off those rough American edges.

Is that a prince I see down there?

STEP THREE:

In Paris, get a fancy new wardrobe. Paris is also where you'll enjoy parties, concerts, and even a flirtation or two, before being officially launched in society as a debutante—a young woman available for marriage.

STEP FOUR:

London is calling! Have your family rent the swankiest house you can find. (Best neighborhood: Mayfair or Belgravia. Prefer hotels? Claridge's will do.) Publicize your arrival with a notice in the society section of a newspaper.

Pleased to meet you, Your Majesty!

STEP FIVE:

Get presented at court to Bertie's mama, Queen Victoria. You'll wear a short-sleeved white gown with a long train, and a long white plume in your hair. Once Vicky nods your way, you're officially "out" in society as a debutante.

STEP SIX:

Ready, set, go! The marriage market known as the London Season begins. While Parliament is in session from May through August, you'll enjoy a whirl of balls, concerts, and other events designed to show you off. If all goes as planned, you'll be engaged before your dancing shoes get scuffed. The Season gave couples just enough time to become infatuated, but not enough time to think twice—like shopping at a mall fifteen minutes before closing.

STEP SEVEN:

Success! OR Failure!

Your aristocrat pops the question. Time for the lawyers to get busy—negotiating your dowry could be as complicated as a royal alliance.

No engagement. Consider participating in the "little Season," when Parliament meets anew in December. Or winter in Paris and return to London to try your luck again at next year's Season.

leading a historian to observe that dowries had become the primary American export.

What led to the Dollar Princesses' warm reception overseas? European royals had plenty of castles but were short on cash; the Industrial Revolution had depleted many estates of farming income. To further complicate matters, the rule of primogeniture meant Eldest Son Inherited All when it came to estates. Younger sons were left desperate for income.

It also helped that the Dollar Princesses' entrance into European society was smiled upon by the Prince of Wales—aka Bertie to his nearest and dearest.

DOLLAR PRINCESSES TAKE EUROPE

As a result of his New York visit, the Prince of Wales decided he liked American women; he'd been charmed by their extroverted ways, which were very different from the proper English ladies at home. With little to do while he waited for mama—Queen Victoria—to depart the throne, the prince filled his days with parties and flirtations to which his wife, Princess Alexandra, turned a blind eye.

The Dollar Princesses kept Bertie entertained. They were charming, beautiful,

Prince Bertie loved New York.

and dressed in the most expensive gowns. They also had money to burn for parties and other frivolities. Unlike Mrs. Astor and her disapproving Four Hundred, Bertie happily welcomed them into the most exclusive drawing rooms of Europe, granting the girls access to royal husbands. Other aristocrats followed suit.

One of Prince Bertie's favorite American ladies was *Lady Jennie Churchill* (1854–1921), the wife of Lord Randolph Churchill, second son of the Duke of Marlborough. Born Jennie Jerome in Brooklyn, she differed from other Dollar Princesses in that her main possession was beauty and charm: Her father, Leonard, had gained and lost four fortunes. Even so, the Jeromes remained wealthy enough that Jennie's mother, Clara, took her three daughters to Paris, where they were welcomed by the court of Empress Eugenie and Napoleon III.

When Prussia invaded France in 1870, Jennie's family fled to England. It was there that Jennie encountered Lord Randolph Churchill at a ball in 1873 in honor of the Prince and Princess of Wales. It was a case of love at first sight. Three days later, the couple was secretly engaged. Once Jennie revealed the match to her father, he enthused in a letter that he was "delighted more than I can tell. It is magnificent. The greatest match any American has made since the Dutchess [sic] of Leeds." Randolph's parents were not as thrilled. If their son was going to marry a vulgar American, she should at least be a really rich vulgar American.

Lady Jennie Churchill at her most glamorous.

To discourage their union, the Duke and Duchess of Marlborough set up countless roadblocks. They insisted Randolph get elected to the House of Commons—a nineteenth-century version of getting a job—before they'd agree to the match. Once Randolph was in the House, lawyers bickered over Jennie's dowry. The duke and duchess were horrified the Jeromes could spare only 50,000 pounds (which would be worth about $6,000,000 in 2017!) for the privilege of marrying into their blue-blooded family.

It appeared true love would not conquer all until Prince Bertie intervened to give his royal approval of the match. The couple finally wed in Paris in April 1874. Years later, Bertie bragged to Jennie's son, Winston Churchill, "You wouldn't be here if it weren't for me." It was a good thing for England, too, that Winston was there: He served as prime minister during one of England's darkest hours, World War II.

After all this drama, did Lady Jennie and her lord live happily ever after? The answer is complicated.

The first years of their marriage were blissful. Two sons were born in rapid succession. Randolph became a firebrand politician, whose ambitions Jennie eagerly supported by campaigning for him. Her work on behalf of medical aid to women in India won her an award from Queen Victoria. But Randolph's worsening health led to eccentric behavior at home and work, causing problems. Just as he was on the brink of becoming prime minister, he quit politics. Nine years later, he was dead. He was only forty-five.

Jennie bounced back, remaining as glamorous in widowhood as she had been in marriage. Suitors clamored for her hand. She refused everyone except George Cornwallis-West, who was half her age. After Cornwallis-West left her for an actress, Jennie married a third and final time to another younger man, Montagu Porch. She joked they would work out as a couple because he had a future and she had a past.

Jennie's passion for fashion proved her undoing: She slipped down a staircase while wearing new Italian slippers. Instead of losing a shoe like Cinderella, Jennie broke an ankle. Her new husband fretted she'd never be able to dance again, but the worst of her trials were to come. Within two weeks, gangrene set in, requiring the amputation of Jennie's leg. As a result, she bled to death—an unfortunate case of death by shoes.

If the shoe doesn't fit, don't wear it.

FOR MONEY, NOT LOVE

Lady Jennie Churchill fared better with her royal marriage than another Dollar Princess, *Consuelo Vanderbilt* (1877–1964). Consuelo wed Charles Spencer-Churchill, better known as the Duke of Marlborough, in 1895. Alas, hers was a union based on money, not love.

The duke, nicknamed Sunny, was the nephew of Jennie Churchill's hubby, Lord Randolph; Consuelo married into the family twenty years after Jennie. As her nuptials approached, royal-wedding fever gripped New York. The press proclaimed Consuelo's engagement to Sunny as the match of the century. The *New York World* reported:

"Miss Consuelo Vanderbilt is one of the greatest heiresses in America. The Duke of Marlborough is probably the most eligible peer in Great Britain . . . From the standpoint of Fifth Avenue it will be the most desirable alliance ever made by an American heiress up to date."

The *New York Times* claimed Consuelo's dowry may have been as much as 20 million dollars, most of which went to fix up Blenheim, Sunny's family palace in England. It was rumored Blenheim was so huge that it took a year to wash all the windows; once the window cleaner arrived at one end of the palace, he simply turned around and started over!

When Consuelo's wedding day arrived, thousands lined Fifth Avenue in Manhattan to the church where she was to tie the knot. Three hundred police were deployed to control the crowds. Drama ensued when the bride arrived twenty minutes late, her tear-stained face hidden behind a heavy veil—but they weren't tears of happiness.

You had to pity Consuelo—she was trapped from the start. Her mother, Alva Vanderbilt, had intended for the girl to marry a royal before she was even born. Alva named Consuelo after Consuelo Yznaga, an heiress who'd wed an English viscount a year before her daughter's birth in a publicity-nabbing wedding. This was only the start of Alva's wheeling and dealing on her daughter's behalf.

When Consuelo was a child, Alva manipulated Mrs. Astor into acknowledging their non-Four Hundred family by throwing an over-the-top costume ball; Alva dressed up as a Venetian princess, like out of a fairy tale from Straparola's *Le piacevoli notti*. To give Consuelo the

Consuelo Vanderbilt. A duchess in the dumps.

posture of a queen, the girl was forced to wear a steel brace from head to hip. She was educated with private governesses, and force-fed music and language lessons. If Consuelo objected, Alva scolded, "I do the thinking, you do as you are told."

When it was time to launch Consuelo into society as a debutante, Alva brought her to Paris, then to London for the Season despite Mrs. Astor's acceptance of their family. Frankly, given all Alva's scheming, it was only a matter of time before Consuelo was seated next to Sunny at a dinner party. Their hostess knew he *had* to marry someone wealthy and cultured—Blenheim was losing two thousand pounds per year. Consuelo was beautiful, educated, and charming. Most important, she was rich.

Alva was thrilled at the match, even if Sunny's desire for Consuelo was mainly mercenary. Consuelo was less excited. She was madly in love with a commoner back in America named Winthrop Rutherfurd, who returned her affection. When Alva found out, she denounced Rutherfurd as a fortune hunter (though he was from a blue-blooded family of his own) and threatened to kill him. When this didn't change Consuelo's mind, Alva claimed a heart attack, so her daughter gave up the man she loved to marry a nobleman who only loved her money. She later wrote of that fateful November day that made her a duchess: "I spent the morning of my wedding day in tears and alone. . . . I felt cold and numb as I went down to meet my father and the bridesmaids who were waiting for me."

Consuelo's life as wife of the Duke of Marlborough was as miserable as she had feared. Eleven years later, after Consuelo provided Sunny with his "heir and a spare," she fled Blenheim. The marriage was eventually annulled in 1926. At the hearing, Alva surprised everyone by testifying she'd forced her daughter to marry Sunny. When push came to shove, motherly instinct trumped Alva's need for a royal in the family.

Once she was freed of her duke, Consuelo married again, this time for love instead of a title. Still, you can take the duchess from the palace, but you can't take the palace from the duchess: Consuelo arranged to be buried near Blenheim upon her death.

AN UNEXPECTED HAPPILY EVER AFTER

Not all "cash for titles" marriages ended as unhappily as Duchess Consuelo's. The fate of *Winnaretta Singer* (1865–1943), an heiress to the Singer sewing machine fortune, offers a bittersweet contrast. She even got to be a real princess.

Winnie's life featured a grand haul of two French princes. Prince #1 was Louis-Vilfred de Scey-Montbéliard, whom she married to escape a violent stepfather. Their wedding night did not go well. When the prince entered the honeymoon suite, Winnie brandished an umbrella against him and shouted, "If you touch me, I'll kill you!"

Regardless, Winnie *liked* being a princess. Her royal title allowed her to indulge her love of art and music. A gifted painter and pianist, she held salons where she presented the music of Debussy, Fauré, Chabrier, and other composers to aristocratic audiences.

By 1892, her loathing of the prince outweighed the positives of princesshood. Princess Winnie ended her marriage the same way Consuelo had: annulment.

A princess no more, Winnie found her music salons snubbed by Parisian society. A husband was needed—and quick. But by then, Winnie had realized she preferred the romantic companionship of women to men. Luckily, her second prince was a far better match, though he initially seemed a risky proposition.

Prince Edmond de Polignac was nearly double her age and desperate for cash after losing everything in unwise business deals. He was prone to unexplainable illnesses that led some to consider him a hypochondriac—a person who imagines him- or herself to be sick when they aren't. However, like Winnie, he loved music (he was a composer) and was more interested in men than women. He wrote in a letter about marrying her: "Our artistic interests will mutually benefit each other, and I hope to be able to make [Winnie] very happy with the admiration that we both have for art." When their engagement was announced, a friend joked, "The sewing machine is going to marry the lyre."

To the surprise of many, their marriage was a roaring success. A princess again, Winnie's music salons regained their audiences. She used them to champion her husband's music, which she genuinely admired. Winnie exhibited her paintings in public, winning praise. The couple grew to love each other deeply. Edmond wrote to Winnie after their marriage: "It is good, rare, and precious to know someone understands you." The couple loved to travel, especially to Venice, where Winnie surprised Edmond by purchasing a palazzo where he could compose music in peace.

It seemed Winnie and her prince would live happily ever after, but Edmond's health, always delicate, soon turned for the worse. He died eight years after their wedding.

Winnie was overcome by sorrow, but she used her tears for good. On the tenth anniversary of his death, the princess established the Fondation Singer-Polignac to honor her husband's memory. Its many philanthropic endeavors include a public housing project in Paris, one of the first of its kind. 👑

Winnaretta Singer.
Muse and musician extraordinaire.

When Consuelo Vanderbilt married the Duke of Marlborough, article after article appeared in newspapers and magazines about everything from Consuelo's bridal flowers to the clothing in her trousseau. (A trousseau is the possessions a bride brings to her new home: clothing, linens, and other household items. Unlike a dowry, the trousseau is for her personal use.) Even the girl's measurements were considered fair game. The *New York World* newspaper went so far as to list Consuelo's weight (116.5 lbs), her waist size (twenty inches), and other private info. "I read to my stupefaction that my garters had gold clasps studded with diamonds," Consuelo recounted in her memoir, *The Glitter and the Gold*.

You might be wondering, "How did the press learn all this? Did they spy on Consuelo?" The truth was, they didn't need to: Mama Alva was often the secret source leaking scoops to reporters.

To be fair, Alva was feeding an established market—stories of heiresses marrying royals were already big news. Two examples: Nearly twenty years earlier, Consuelo's namesake, Consuelo Yznaga, caused an eruption of newspaper headlines when she married the viscount-*slash*-future Duke of Mandeville in New York City in 1876. Mary Leiter's 1895 marriage to George Curzon also won press attention, especially after the bride became a baroness and vicereine of India in 1898. (Vicereine was the highest court position a British woman could hold in colonial India—quite the royal leap of rank for American-born Mary!)

Just as we read *People* or *Us Weekly* today for glimpses of celebrity life, it's easy to imagine a turn-of-the-century girl reading about the Dollar Princesses, visions of golden corsets and diamond tiaras dancing in her head—Cinderella for a new age.

HELP WANTED: Good fairy to reverse the curse. Apply immediately.

CHAPTER 6:

When the Tiara Doesn't Fit

"A marriage is no amusement but a solemn act, and generally a sad one."

—Queen Victoria (1819–1901)

The Dollar Princess marriages marked a turning point for those who'd considered "Cinderella" only a fairy tale. Royalty was no longer something you had to be born into. Instead, it became a commodity that anyone could gain with enough money and the right social connections. All you had to do was get married.

Most of these "cash for titles" unions didn't differ much from a traditional royal alliance: Their function was to consolidate power and money. Affection was beside the point.

Even without love, the allure of a title through marriage was hard to

A PLETHORA OF PRINCESSES

In 1907, the *New York Times* reported that twenty-seven American girls had become princesses through marriage by that year. Besides Winnaretta Singer, they included:

Julia Dent Grant, a granddaughter of President Ulysses S. Grant. She married Prince Cantacuzene of Russia.

Alice Heine, a daughter of a New Orleans banker. She married the Prince of Monaco, the monarch of a tiny principality in the southern part of France.

Clara Ward, the daughter of a Detroit multimillionaire. She married a Belgian prince only to dump him for a traveling violinist. (More about Clara later.)

resist for socially striving Americans. British titles bore the highest value due to scarcity. *Titled Americans*, an 1890 husband-hunting guide for American heiresses, explained there were not more than three thousand persons bearing titles in Great Britain; of these, only thirty were dukes at that time. If you traveled across the Channel to the Continent, the field got wider. There were even princes available for those heiresses yearning to be a *real* princess.

These titles held less prestige than you'd expect. *Titled Americans* stated, "There are hundreds, nay thousands, of so-called Princes [in Russia]. . . . Their title of Prince is due to a misapprehension and wrong translation." In France, "[t]he eldest son of a Duke should assume during his father's lifetime the title of Prince."

In other words, marrying a prince didn't lead to a throne—but it did mean the prince got an infusion of cold, hard American cash to accompany his princess bride.

The gilded age of the Dollar Princess "cash for titles" marriages whimpered to a close with the start of the first World War in 1914. Even before then, the press had begun to report on the darker side of Marrying Royal.

Once word got out that American heiresses came with a big, fat dowry, impoverished European nobles didn't bother with the social niceties of the London Season. Instead, they crossed the Atlantic to come a-courting. In 1895, a founder of the National Association of Manufacturers complained that the British "come over here and trade us a second-class duke or a third-class earl for a first-class American girl, and get several million dollars to boot." An 1888 *New York Times* headline proclaimed of an American heiress marrying a French duke, "She Pays All the Bills—He Thinks Himself Cheap at the Price." The bride was Isabelle Blanche Singer, Winnaretta's younger sister. In a sad turn of events, Isabelle died mysteriously of cardiac arrest at the age of twenty-seven; some thought she'd committed suicide.

It didn't help the reputation of these transatlantic unions that Consuelo Vanderbilt and Winnaretta Singer weren't alone in finding royal married life a real downer. After their exciting debutante seasons and highly publicized weddings, most Dollar Princess brides were exiled to country estates far from family and friends, who remained an ocean away in the United States. If that wasn't depressing enough, their husbands' Old World homes were downright medieval compared to the luxurious New World mansions their plutocrat daddies had built back home.

Want a hot bath? Forget about modern plumbing, where hot water is available with a twist of the wrist. Instead, ring a servant to carry water from the kitchen. Feeling cold? Put on another shawl. Better yet, cough up even more money to have central heating installed. After all, it was the Dollar Princess's responsibility to modernize her royal husband's out-of-date estate—that's why she'd been wed in the first place.

Despite scandal, a few Dollar Princess wives abandoned their aristocratic husbands, just as Consuelo and Winnie had. (Better to live

Clara Ward. A very theatrical princess.

without a tiara than live with tears!) However, for Michigan heiress *Clara Ward* (1873–1916), life without her prince didn't go as planned.

RECIPE FOR A SCANDAL

At first glance, Clara Ward appeared to have all her ducks in a row. She was beautiful. She was charming. She had a millionaire father who died when Clara was a toddler, leaving her with a massive inheritance. Clara's mother possessed the wisdom to have her daughter debut in London, rather than remain in their hometown of Detroit or try their luck in New York.

All appeared to be going according to plan when Clara tied the knot with Marie Joseph Anatole Pierre Alphonse de Riquet, the Prince de Caraman Chimay. At their 1890 wedding in Paris, the middle-aged Belgian prince owned little save his title; in other words, he was one of those fortune hunters the American press complained about. Even so, the alliance was considered a good match for the seventeen-year-old heiress.

It was no surprise that Clara's money immediately went to fixing up the prince's chateau and paying off his debts. She promptly gave birth to a daughter and a son. (Again, all part of the plan.)

Then, suddenly, nothing went as planned.

One night in December 1896 while the prince slept, the princess crept out of her bed. She was later joined by a man who wasn't her husband—a traveling violinist named Rigó Jancsi she'd met just over a week earlier at a restaurant in Paris.

The *Times* of Philadelphia described Rigó as "anything but an Adonis, being skinny, awkward, pitted with smallpox." Regardless, the two fell madly in love at first sight.

Years later, Rigó described their fateful first meeting at the restaurant:

"She was the most beautiful woman in all Europe. Kings loved her. The night I saw her first she turned from King Leopold to smile at me. Ten days later, like two gypsies, we stole from her palace in the dead of night, and I took her to my mother's hut in the mountains near Pakozd, where I was born."

From then on, things progressed rather quickly on the scandal front.

In January, a mere month after they'd eloped, passionate love gave way to raucous quarrels in a Milan hotel; Clara took off without Rigó, leaving him scrambling to pay his half of the bill. By February, Rigó and Clara had reconciled and the prince sued for divorce; he won cash and custody of their children once the princess confessed all. In March, Clara and Rigó announced they'd be appearing at the Wintergarten theater in Berlin. In April, the head of the police threatened to expel her from France if she went onstage in Paris.

Later that same year, police forbade the sale of photographs of the princess; the racy photos revealed Clara's tattoo of the Chimay crown, a leftover from her royal marriage. Retailers trashed thousands of the highly profitable photographs, which only increased public demand—*everyone* wanted to see the princess who'd dumped a prince.

It took Rigó and the princess over a year to marry because Rigó already had a wife. Some have speculated that Clara faked her own death to force him to get a divorce. After her miraculous return to life, the princess took to the stage to cash in on the scandal, posing in daringly skintight flesh-colored costumes that made her look as though she were naked.

Like her first, this marriage did not last. Nor did Clara's inheritance; by 1901, her family had intervened to have her declared incapable of managing her property. Rigó bragged that the princess had bought him "a white marble palace on the Nile. An Italian architect designed the stables for the sixteen jet-black Arabian horses she bought for me. . . . She gave me my $5,000 violin and caskets of jewels."

Clara's adventures continued until her death in Italy in 1916. Newspapers reported the princess was buried in a pauper's coffin. However, Clara had one last surprise up her sleeve: Her will revealed an estate of over a million dollars, most of which was left in a trust for her son and daughter from her first marriage. Turned out she'd saved money all along from her time on the stage.

Also left behind: a recipe for a dessert that bears her violinist's name. The origin of Rigó Jancsi cake is as murky as his Hungarian past; his name translates into English as "Johnny Blackbird." It's believed Rigó asked a baker friend in Budapest to invent the cake for his princess bride. Two facts are certain: The cake is baked of chocolate as dark as a blackbird's wing, and it tastes like chocolate mousse cake. Yum!

THE BARONESS: DADA'S MAMA

*"The Baroness"
Famous model from
New York puts Art
into posing. . . .*

— *from an advertisement
by the Baroness
Elsa von Freytag-
Loringhoven*

The Baroness in motion.

Around the same time Clara was throwing caution to the wind, the *Baroness Elsa von Freytag-Loringhoven* (1874–1927) arrived on the scene, using her noble name to win attention as a model and for her sculptures, paintings, and collages. Elsa was also a gifted poet, able to turn something as simple as an advertisement into an artistic statement.

Like Clara Ward, Baroness Elsa gained her noble title from marriage. Unlike Clara, she was no Dollar Princess—Elsa came from a humble Polish-German family with a history of mental illness. Elsa's father was a violent, alcoholic bricklayer; her mother had tried to kill herself. If that wasn't bad enough, Elsa's paternal grandfather was an alcoholic while her paternal grandmother was rumored to be a kleptomaniac—someone unable to stop herself from stealing things.

It was no surprise when Elsa clashed with her father, which led to her running away to Berlin in 1893. To survive, she became an artist's model. Soon she was making art herself with considerable accomplishment.

Eventually, Elsa made her way back across the Atlantic to New York City, where she wed the Baron Leopold Freiherr von Freytag-Loringhoven in 1913. She was thirty-nine and had married three times previously; the Baron was eleven years younger and from a distinguished aristocratic family.

The royal couple possessed romantic chemistry and little else. Leopold had served as a Prussian military officer but ruined his career due to debt. Desperate for a new start, he traveled to America, where he ended up employed as a busboy. Regardless, Elsa looked upon her new royal title as a way to declare herself artistic aristocracy to the world. Soon she was touting herself as "the Baroness" to anyone who'd listen.

A year after the wedding, World War I broke out. The Baron hightailed it back to Europe without the Baroness, stealing her scant savings. (So much for loyal royals!) Now *really* bankrupt, Elsa returned to modeling. She also made sculptures out of garbage, anticipating the avant-garde Dada art movement to come.

Marcel Duchamp, an artist associated with Dada, revolutionized the art world by creating readymade "sculptures" out of everyday objects such as bicycle wheels or a snow shovel. The Baroness went one step further: She turned herself into art.

She wore teaspoons as earrings and postal stamps on her cheeks. She dressed herself in tomato cans and draped a taillight over her rear end. She explained, "Cars and bicycles have taillights. Why not I?" She shaved her head and painted her scalp with red shellac. The author Djuna Barnes described Elsa as "strange with beauty." But the Baroness's continuing mental instabilities cost her her friends, leading her to abandon America in 1923.

Elsa's situation improved once she arrived in Paris, where she launched herself again as an artist's model and set up a studio. She wrote to Peggy Guggenheim, a collector of modern art, to request a grant for her modeling-as-art endeavor, and made a friend at a gallery. Then a new problem arrived, which set the always volatile Baroness into panic mode. Her visa status prohibited her from working in France, and she fretted she'd be deported.

It all came to an end one stormy December day in 1927 in the City of Lights. Baroness Elsa's body was discovered on her bed, like Sleeping Beauty without a good fairy to save her. Someone had forgotten to turn off the gas in her cheap apartment, and she'd died of carbon monoxide poisoning.

Was her death a suicide—or a tragic accident? No one knows for sure, though one fact suggests accident: The corpse of Elsa's favorite dog, Pinky, was found beside her. As crazy as Elsa may have been, those who knew her believed she loved animals too much to knowingly harm one.

TWO TRAGIC PRINCESSES

Baroness Elsa wasn't alone in meeting an untimely end despite having a royal title. As she learned the hard way, nobility can't fix what's broken. For two other female royals it was politics, rather than madness, that cost them their lives.

Princess Mafalda of Savoy (1902–1944) was a daughter of the king of Italy. Her marriage to Prince Philipp of Hesse was touted as a great way to align German and Italian political interests; he was the second member of his family to marry into the House of Savoy, further strengthening the two countries' ties. The prince was a member of the National Socialist German Workers' Party, better known as the Nazi party. (Yup, *those* Nazis.)

Fast forward four children and nearly two decades of marriage later: In 1943, Hitler had Prince Philipp arrested and sent Princess Mafalda to Buchenwald concentration camp. Hitler had denounced Mafalda as the "blackest carrion in the Italian royal house." Whether or not the couple was involved with anti-Nazi activities, their imprisonment was Germany's way of getting the Italian royal family out of their way after Italy had broken from the Axis, a formal alliance Italy made with Germany and Japan in 1936.

Princess Mafalda died in the camp in 1944 as a result of injuries from a bomb. Before she breathed her last, it was rumored she said to other Italian inmates, "Remember me not as an Italian princess, but as an Italian sister."

Some forty years earlier, *Princess Ka'iulani of Hawaii*

Princess Mafalda
before her troubles.

(1875–1899) was also muscled out of power. Ka'iulani had been first in line to the Hawaiian throne until the monarchy was overthrown in 1893; it was all part of an American plan to annex Hawaii. Upon learning the worst, the crown princess protested, "Have I done anything wrong that this wrong should be done to me and my people?"

Until then, Ka'iulani's life had been peaceful. She spent her childhood on an idyllic estate in Waikiki, where she was fond of feeding the peacocks that lived there. She left Hawaii at fourteen to be educated in Great Britain, and proved herself to be a gifted scholar and artist.

Life in exile wasn't easy. Those in favor of the United States annexing Hawaii claimed Ka'iulani was uncivilized despite her education and talents. To counter their racism and to encourage the restoration of her crown, the princess traveled around America and Europe on a massive public relations tour. She spoke persuasively to the press:

"Today, I, a poor weak girl with not one of my people with me and all these Hawaiian statesmen against me, have strength to stand up for the rights of my people. Even now I can hear their wail in my heart and it gives me strength and courage and I am strong."

It seemed that all might be set right—Ka'iulani convinced President Cleveland to speak on her behalf—but Congress refused to restore the Hawaiian monarchy, and American annexation occurred in 1898.

Ka'iulani was heartbroken. Soon after, she got sick after horseback riding in a storm. Within a few months, death robbed the princess of her throne as surely as politics had stolen her land. 👑

Princess Ka'iulani.

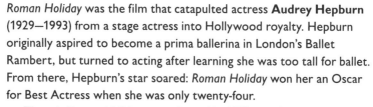

Roman Holiday was the film that catapulted actress **Audrey Hepburn** (1929–1993) from a stage actress into Hollywood royalty. Hepburn originally aspired to become a prima ballerina in London's Ballet Rambert, but turned to acting after learning she was too tall for ballet. From there, Hepburn's star soared: *Roman Holiday* won her an Oscar for Best Actress when she was only twenty-four.

Though *Roman Holiday* was released in 1953, its plot appears to be influenced by history: The film involves a princess running away to escape the unyielding responsibilities of the throne. Hepburn played the role of Ann, a young princess from an unnamed European country. During an over-scheduled publicity tour of Rome, Ann escapes from her bedroom to explore the Eternal City in disguise. During her adventures, she encounters a handsome American journalist who soon figures out the princess's identity. The journalist's hunger for an exclusive scoop becomes complicated by his growing affection for Ann. Ultimately, to protect her from scandal, he decides to keep his lips zipped about her Roman holiday—and poor Ann returns to her unhappy life as a princess. The film is still popular today, and was selected by the Library of Congress's National Film Registry for preservation in 1999; the National Film Registry works to ensure the continued availability of American films that are culturally, historically, or artistically important.

Princess Audrey having fun in Rome.

Princess? Heroine? BOTH!

CHAPTER 7

Princesses for Everyone

> "Being a princess isn't all it's cracked up to be."
>
> — Diana, Princess of Wales (1961–1997)

Today, the original definition of a princess—the blue-blooded daughter of a king and queen—has been transformed almost beyond recognition into a "pretty in pink" role model for girls. The popularity of princesses was encouraged by the Disney Princess brand, which was founded in 2000 and reached annual sales of 5.5 billion dollars by 2015. Andy Mooney, the brand's creator, had a "eureka" moment after noticing little girls wearing homemade princess costumes at a Disney on Ice event. Mooney asked their mothers, "If we made this, would you buy it?" From there, it was only a hop, skip, and factory order to flood stores with Cinderella tiaras and Sleeping Beauty sleeping bags.

Other companies followed suit with princess products targeted to girls: LEGO, Dora the Explorer, Barbie, and more.

Princesses aren't only for the ten-and-under set. Tweens and teens devoured Meg Cabot's *The Princess Diaries* and its sequels, along with the film versions starring Anne Hathaway. Shannon Hale's Princess Academy books added to the growing genre, and her Princess in Black series revamped the royal role model for a younger generation.

In addition, changing technology has encouraged our fascination with royalty. Sales of televisions skyrocketed before the 1953 televised coronation of Great Britain's Queen Elizabeth II; the three-hour ceremony was viewed by an estimated 20 million people in Great Britain, and another 85 million in the United States. In 1969, the Queen allowed cameras to film her domestic life like a reality show. The result was a television documentary entitled *Royal Family*, which famed broadcaster Sir David Attenborough claimed was "killing the monarchy" by making the Queen and her family seem too much like us. A generation later, the fairy tale wedding of Elizabeth's eldest son, Prince Charles, to Lady Diana Spencer, better known as *Princess Diana*, was watched by 750 million people worldwide.

But soon there was a dark side to this unprecedented media access: scandal.

If televising the Windsor family sparked the modern obsession with royalty, the paparazzi fanned that spark into a fire. Paparazzi—freelance celebrity photographers—stalked the royals day and night, hoping to photograph them doing something newsworthy. The photographs would then be sold at great profit to newspapers and magazines.

The paparazzi's favorite target? Prince Charles's first wife, Princess Diana. In time, their pursuit would take a deadly turn.

Diana was only nineteen in 1980 when her romance with Charles transformed her from a posh-but-humble nursery school teacher into the most talked about woman in the world. Diana, who'd met Charles as a young girl, had bought into the whole "I want to marry a prince" dream big time; she'd even told a friend that marrying Charles "could be quite fun. It would be like Anne Boleyn or Guinevere!" In a way, yearning for a royal true love was in Diana's blood: Georgiana, the Duchess of Devonshire, was a distant ancestor.

It was a dream come true for Diana when the prince proposed. But Diana's dream turned into a nightmare when the press wouldn't leave her alone.

Once Diana and Charles said "I do," the public's interest only intensified. Paparazzi photographed the new princess in her bathing suit less than a year after the wedding. They cornered her at clubs partying with other royals and friends. They spied on Diana sweating at the gym. After the princess became a mother, the press interrupted outings with her two sons, ignoring pleas from Buckingham Palace to grant them privacy.

Unsurprisingly, Diana unraveled under the constant surveillance—it was like living in a tiny fishbowl. It didn't help that soon after her wedding, she discovered Charles still had the hots for his ex Camilla. Overwhelmed, her life spun out of control. She developed an eating disorder

The Wives of Windsor
A Family Tree

In 1952, Queen Elizabeth II of the royal House of Windsor ascended the British throne and has ruled ever since. Her 1947 marriage to Prince Philip, the Duke of Edinburgh, produced one daughter and three sons. Though the Queen has reigned with little scandal, Prince Charles and his two wives have provided the press with much to write about. Here's an overview of Elizabeth's immediate family:

Queen Elizabeth II
(b. 1926)

Prince Philip, the Duke of Edinburgh
(b. 1921)

PRINCE CHARLES
(b. 1948)

PRINCESS ANNE
(b. 1950)

PRINCE ANDREW
(b. 1960)

PRINCE EDWARD
(b. 1964)

PRINCESS DIANA. A MOST TRAGIC PRINCESS.

When **Diana, Princess of Wales** (1961–1997), married Prince Charles in 1981, she bore the nickname "Shy Di." Within a decade, she became one of the most glamorous women in the world—and one of the unhappiest. Charles was still in love with an old flame who'd married another man. To avenge herself, Diana spilled the beans on their marriage in a tell-all BBC television interview in 1995. After the divorce, Diana remained a princess but lost the title of Her Royal Highness because she was no longer in line to the throne.

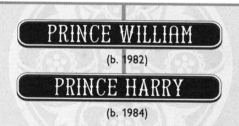

PRINCE WILLIAM
(b. 1982)

PRINCE HARRY
(b. 1984)

Camilla, Duchess of Cornwall (b. 1947), was the "old flame" Prince Charles still loved while married to Diana. In 1992, transcripts of her lovey-dovey telephone conversations with Prince Charles were read by millions after they were published in newspapers. Camilla divorced her husband and became Charles's second wife in 2005. Out of respect for Diana, Camilla will instead adopt the title of Princess Consort when Charles becomes king.

and revealed her disappointments with her marriage in a TMI television interview.

After what seemed like an inevitable divorce in 1996, Diana turned her energy toward charity work, using her fame to further awareness of AIDS, land mines, and other worthy causes. Hoping to create a new life, she begged the press for breathing room. Her request went ignored with tragic results.

On a hot July night in Paris, Princess Diana was killed in a car accident while being pursued by paparazzi on motorcycles. Her driver, who'd had too much to drink, had been speeding to evade them.

Even as Diana lay dying, the press circled like vultures. Within minutes of the crash, the first paparazzo on the scene had sold exclusive photographs of the fatally injured princess to a tabloid for 300,000 pounds.

At her funeral, Diana's brother summed up her life:

> "[O]f all the ironies about Diana, perhaps the greatest was this—a girl given the name of the ancient goddess of hunting, was in the end, the most hunted person of the modern age."

THE OTHER SIDE OF THE CAMERA

The untimely death of Princess Diana revealed the dark side of the modern princess dream. It's hard to imagine anyone surviving under such scrutiny. A generation earlier, though, *Princess Grace of*

Monaco (1929–1982) had a friendlier relationship with the camera: Before marrying her prince, she'd gained fame as a movie star under her maiden name, Grace Kelly.

Grace hailed from a Philadelphia family wealthy enough to have a mansion and a chauffeur. But she had aspirations beyond social stature— she yearned to act. Luckily, the camera loved her. Famed film director John Ford proclaimed, "This dame has breeding, quality, class." Ford was right: By 1955, she'd won the Academy Award for Best Actress for her role in *The Country Girl*.

Though Grace made only eleven films, her cool blonde beauty made an indelible impression on the world. She was the classy girl next door, a dream that could never be attained. In short, Grace Kelly was *it*.

Looking back, Grace's next-to-last film, *The Swan*, seemed a rehearsal for what was to be the biggest role of her life. In *The Swan*, Grace played the princess of an unspecified European country. Within a month after finishing the film, she was engaged to Prince Rainier III of Monaco, a small principality located in the southern part of France.

(How small is Monaco? Less-than-one-square-mile small. Only-20,000-subjects small. A train-stop-on-the-way-to-France small. That small.)

Cynics claimed Grace and Rainier's engagement seemed fishy, especially after he nabbed a 2-million-dollar dowry from Grace and her well-to-do father. Did Rainier love Grace? Or did he love the glamour she brought Monaco? Until Grace came along, Monaco's main claim to fame was its casino; *Life* magazine described the principality as "largely ignored throughout its long history." After Grace, *everyone* knew where Monaco was. In addition, the prince needed an heir, or Monaco would revert to French rule.

As for Grace, had she married the prince because she'd tired of Hollywood? Or was she Marrying Royal, like the Dollar Princesses had a half century earlier? Alfred Hitchcock, who'd directed her in *Rear Window* and *To Catch a Thief*, stated that she had found "the best role of her life." Whatever the truth, one fact is certain: Grace and Rainier's 1956 royal nuptials were proclaimed the wedding of the century, just as Consuelo Vanderbilt's wedding had been in the nineteenth century.

Life imitated art as cameras surrounded Grace and Rainier while they took their vows, which were televised to over thirty million people in a dozen countries. Additional cameras gathered

Princess Grace. Always graceful.

footage for a short documentary, *The Wedding in Monaco*, which was distributed by Grace's film studio; the royal couple received a cut of the profits. The wedding documentary was to be Grace's last official film appearance as a star, for Rainier had forbidden her to return to acting.

The princess moved into her new life with aplomb. She gave birth to three children, including the required male heir, and devoted herself to philanthropy. Her favorite charities supported the arts and provided necessary resources to underprivileged children. She was the model of a modern princess.

But like Princess Diana, Grace's life was cut tragically short. While driving along the winding Riviera roads, she missed a turn and careened 120 feet off a cliff. Though her injuries were fatal, it was discovered she'd suffered a stroke, which may have affected her ability to drive. She was fifty-two.

Princess Grace's 1982 funeral attracted even more eyes than her wedding: Nearly a hundred million people watched it on television. One of the four hundred guests who attended in person was Princess Diana, who'd wed Charles just a year earlier.

* *

Now that we've looked at princesses from both history and story, who's the fairest of them all? Turn the page to find out! 👑

History always wins.
Doesn't it?

TOURNAMENT of

Not in my case,
I fear.

Lucrezia Borgia

vs.

Elizabeth Báthory

Lucrezia Borgia

vs.

Elizabeth Tudor

Mary Tudor

vs.

Elizabeth Tudor

Elizabeth Tudor

Elizabeth posed clothed for her portraits.

Elizabeth Tudor

Louise-Françoise de Bourbon

vs.

Françoise-Marie de Bourbon

Françoise-Marie de Bourbon

vs.

Pauline Bonaparte

Princess de Lambelle

vs.

Pauline Bonaparte

Pauline Bonaparte

Princess Diana

Queen Bess got the throne upgrade. But Diana reigns as queen in our hearts.

Duchess of Devonshire

vs.

Consuelo Vanderbilt

Consuelo Vanderbilt

vs.

Jennie Churchill

Jennie Churchill

vs.

Winnaretta Singer

Jennie Churchill

CINDERELLA WINS!

Cinderella inspired Diana to marry a prince—for better or for worse. Therefore story trumps the harsh reality of history.

Close, but Diana wins because of her royal blood.

Princess Diana

Clara Ward

vs.

Baroness Elsa

Clara Ward

vs.

Princess Diana

Princess Ka'iulani

vs.

Princess Diana

Princess Diana

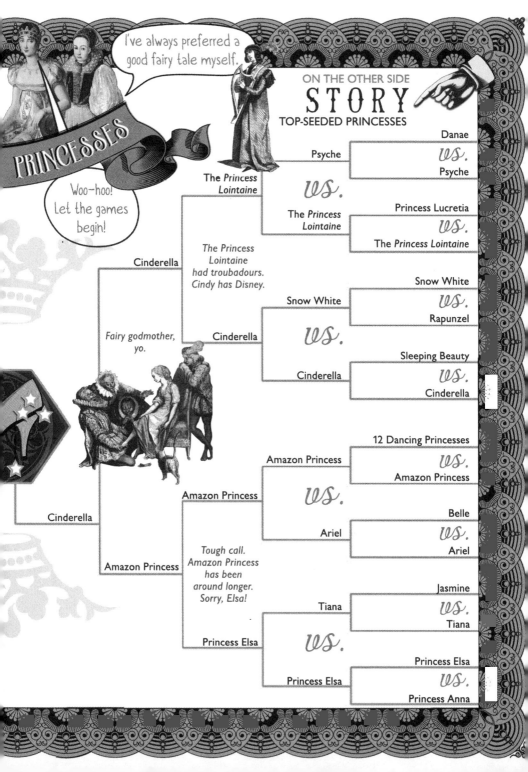

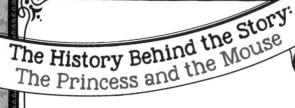

The glamorous lives and untimely deaths of Princess Diana and Princess Grace represent the best and the worst of modern princesshood. Both women used their privilege for good. Both were hailed as international style icons. Both perished in car accidents before their time. Yet when most girls think of princesses, their thoughts usually first turn to Disney Princesses rather than to Diana or Grace. Who was the man whose films inspired the brand?

Walt Disney (1901–1966) began his career as a cartoonist who gained fame from a cute mouse named Mickey. When animating Mickey Mouse wasn't enough of a challenge, Disney devoted four years to creating the first full-length animated film, *Snow White and the Seven Dwarfs.* The film cost more than four times what he'd initially budgeted; at one point, he feared the bank would take over his company. But Disney's gamble paid off when the film became the most successful film of 1938, and won an Academy Award for innovation. *Time* magazine proclaimed it "an authentic masterpiece."

Snow White was Disney's first princess-themed animated movie—but not its last. Since then, over a dozen princesses have joined Snow's ranks, two recent additions being Princesses Elsa and Anna from *Frozen.*

Examined as a whole, the Disney Princess films show how our beliefs about princesses have changed over time. A vice president in charge of licensing at Disney explained, "The Princess franchise has to evolve. The focus will be on empowered heroines."

Reflecting this evolution, the films often differ from the fairy tales that inspired them. Let's take a closer look to see how:

1937: Snow White and the Seven Dwarfs
Based on "Snow White" *(Brothers Grimm, 1812).*

Though Disney kept close to the Grimms' fairy tale, he streamlined the Evil Queen's three attempts to murder Snow into one encounter with a poisoned apple. Otherwise, Snow remains as devoted to housework as she was in the fairy tale—what would those dwarfs have done without her mad cleaning skills?

1950: Cinderella
Based on "Cinderella, or the Little Glass Slipper"
(Charles Perrault, 1697).

Cinderella is just as much a housekeeper as in the fairy tale, but Disney ups the cuteness by giving her mouse friends and a dastardly cat to menace them. Only one ball is held instead of Perrault's three. One surprising change from the fairy tale: Cinderella produces the glass slipper at the end, taking charge of her destiny and her own happily ever after.

1959: Sleeping Beauty
Based on "The Beauty Sleeping in the Wood"
(Charles Perrault, 1697).

Disney's Sleeping Beauty, aka Princess Aurora, gains a memorable adversary in Maleficent, one of the most terrifying villains to ever curse a princess. (Maleficent even got a movie of her own in 2014.) Aurora spends a lot of time singing in the forest. However, Perrault's tale continues after true love's kiss: Sleeping Beauty bears two children, both of whom are nearly eaten by the prince's ogress mother. Nice, Granny! (Not.)

1989: The Little Mermaid
Based on "The Little Mermaid" (Hans Christian Andersen, 1837).

Hans Christian Andersen's Little Mermaid dissolves into ocean foam when her prince marries someone else; Disney's far pluckier Ariel gets to keep the prince *and* her legs. She also gains three comedic sidekicks: a helpful seagull, a musically talented crab, and a nervous fish. Ursula the sea witch tries to stop Ariel's romance with the prince by stealing her voice and turning herself into a beautiful princess.

1991: Beauty and the Beast
Based on "Beauty and the Beast"
(Gabrielle-Suzanne Barbot de Villeneuve, 1740).

Disney morphed Villeneuve's half-royal/half-fairy heroine into Belle, a bookworm with an inventor father. Other departures from the fairy tale: Instead of two greedy sisters undermining Beauty's return to the Beast, Belle is stuck with Gaston, a wannabe boyfriend who's more muscle than brains. Once we get to the Beast's palace, there are dancing teacups and candlesticks. The Beast softens Belle's heart when she gets a load of his awesome library.

2009: The Princess and the Frog
Based on "The Frog Prince; or, Iron Henry"
(Brothers Grimm, 1812).

The parable by the Brothers Grimm about the importance of keeping a promise was transformed by Disney into a comedy-adventure set in twentieth-century New Orleans. Most important, Disney introduced their first African American princess, a spunky aspiring chef named Tiana who works as a waitress. Another big difference: Tiana is turned into a frog when she kisses the Frog Prince instead of the frog turning into a prince as in the Grimms' fairy tale. Confusion abounds before Tiana and her prince regain their human forms. If that's not exciting enough, there's also a lovelorn firefly and lively jazz music.

2010: Tangled
Based on "Rapunzel" (Brothers Grimm, 1812).

In Disney's upside-down reworking of the fairy tale, Rapunzel is already a princess in her own right; she was taken from her royal parents at birth by a witch. Instead of a prince to rescue her, there's a thief named Flynn who's caught looking to steal from her tower. Our girl Rapunzel is a crazy-good artist—hey, she's got time to kill in that tower—and feisty, too. She also has super-long hair that can magically preserve life. After plot twists that have nothing to do with anything Grimm, Flynn cuts off Rapunzel's magical hair to free her from the witch who'd imprisoned her. Afterward, Rapunzel is reunited with her royal family, who never stopped hoping to find her. It's implied that Rapunzel lives happily ever after with Flynn, short hair and all.

2013: Frozen
Based on "The Snow Queen" (Hans Christian Andersen, 1844).

The plot of *Frozen* is barely recognizable from the Andersen fairy tale that served as inspiration. Frankly, it's easier to list the similarities than the differences: There's a snow queen and a lot of snow. (Disappointed? Just Let It Go.)

Becoming a **PRINCESS** isn't the end.
It's the beginning.

Happily Ever After

> "I don't want to be a princess who sits on the sidelines; I want to be present and actively involved. It's a life with a purpose."
>
> —Charlene, Princess of Monaco (b. 1978)

Over a thousand years have passed since medieval troubadours sang of the *princesse lointaine*—the "distant princess" renowned for her beauty and unavailability. Today, many girls' first real-life princess experience was awakening at dawn to watch the televised 2011 wedding of Princess Diana's elder son, William, to Kate Middleton. After marriage, Kate was titled *Catherine, Duchess of Cambridge* (b. 1982).

Unlike William's blue-blooded mum, Diana, Kate comes from a decidedly middle class background: Her mother is a former British Airways flight attendant who started a successful party supply business with Kate's dad. Evidence suggests that the prince chose his bride out of true affection rather than political motivations. Will and Kate met as students at St. Andrew's University in Scotland. Despite a painfully long and public courtship—the tabloids nicknamed her "Waity Katie"—the pretty brunette managed to beat out royals and celebrities to win the heart of Europe's most eligible bachelor. The couple are now the proud parents of Prince George and Princess Charlotte, their "heir and a spare." (The good news: In 2013, the British Succession to the Crown Act was updated to replace male primogeniture with absolute primogeniture. In other words, when it comes to inheriting the British throne, all that matters is who's born first, not gender. Score one for the ladies!)

Kate's Cinderella transformation from school chum to married royal is a remarkable example of how the role of princess has evolved over the centuries. Even before her wedding, Kate showed she was in it for more than the bling. Instead of registering for china, she and the prince set up a bridal gift fund that allowed well-wishers to donate to twenty-six charities. Since then, she has become a patron to numerous philanthropic organizations and works on behalf of her own charity, The Royal Foundation of The Duke and Duchess of Cambridge and Prince Harry.

With these actions, the duchess is treading a well-worn path. Today's royal women are expected to espouse a cause as examples of *noblesse oblige*, a French phrase meaning "to perform good deeds for those less fortunate." William's mother, Princess Diana, campaigned against land mines; Monaco's Princess Grace was a patron of the arts. Their legacies continue to inspire royal women of the twenty-first century.

So who are today's princesses, and what are their causes?

✳ *Princess Sikhanyiso Dlamini* (b. 1987) of Swaziland has taken some heat for rebelling against her country's traditions. Aside from dressing in modern Western clothing, the twenty-something princess also stood up to her father, King Mswati III, by denouncing his polygamy—marriage to more than one woman at a time. In 2013, she launched the Imbali Foundation, which seeks to empower girls in her native land.

✳ *Crown Princess Victoria of Sweden* (b. 1977) used her position to set up the self-titled Crown Princess Victoria Fund. This charitable endeavor provides support for children and young people with functional disabilities or chronic illnesses. She is in line to become Sweden's third queen to rule as regent, and steps in for her father the king when necessary.

✳ On the athletic front, *Maitha bint Mohammed bin Rashid al Maktoum* (b. 1980), a Dubai *sheikha*—a title given to an Arabian royal female—represented the United Arab Emirates in the 2008 Summer Olympics. Her sport of choice? Tae kwon do.

✳ *Charlene, Princess of Monaco* (b. 1978), also a former Olympian, married Princess Grace's son, Albert, in 2011. She devotes energy toward the Princess Grace Foundation, a nonprofit that aids emerging talents in the arts.

✳ Perhaps the most incredible princess story of all belongs to *Sarah Culberson* (b. 1976), whose life bears astonishing similarity to Princess Mia from the fictional *Princess Diaries*. Sarah is an adopted biracial American woman who discovered her biological father was African royalty. Princess Sarah used her new status to create the Kposowa Foundation in 2006, a nonprofit devoted to rebuilding educational resources in the

Bumpe Chiefdom after the Blood Diamond war. The foundation has since been rebranded as Sierra Leone Rising and has expanded its work to include female empowerment and health resources.

More than glorified social queens, these modern royal women reveal how the passive but beautiful *princesse lointaine* adored by troubadours has changed over the centuries into a royal mover-and-shaker who, in some cases, can actually kick butt like Katniss Everdeen.

Princesses have been around for as long as there have been females yearning to be fairest in the land. The challenge for today's girls: Transform the "bad princess" of old into a new force for true female empowerment. As the future of this most feminine of role models is shaped, there's plenty of hope for those who yearn to turn Pretty in Pink into Purposeful in Pink.

But wait! There's more! Turn the page to try your luck at the *Princess Paths to Power* game. (Instructions can be found on pages 124–125.) ♛

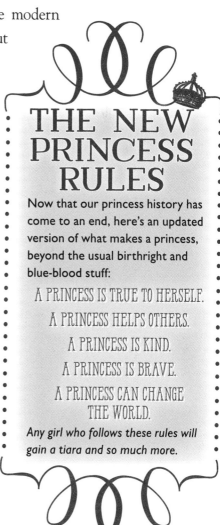

THE NEW PRINCESS RULES

Now that our princess history has come to an end, here's an updated version of what makes a princess, beyond the usual birthright and blue-blood stuff:

A PRINCESS IS TRUE TO HERSELF.

A PRINCESS HELPS OTHERS.

A PRINCESS IS KIND.

A PRINCESS IS BRAVE.

A PRINCESS CAN CHANGE THE WORLD.

Any girl who follows these rules will gain a tiara and so much more.

GAME INSTRUCTIONS

OBJECT OF THE GAME:

Arrive first at the Throne Room to be crowned queen. Two to four princesses may play.

SETUP:

You'll need one die (half a pair of dice) and a small token for each player. Suggested tokens: acorn, rock, button. Each player places her token in the Nursery and rolls the die. The highest roll goes first.

PRINCESS WARS:

When a princess lands on this space, she plays a game of Rock-Paper-Scissors with the first player to her right. The winner gets to jump forward six spaces.

THE DUNGEON:

A princess is sent to the Dungeon if she lands on a space sentencing her accordingly. To free herself, she must roll a six with the die within two turns. If she is unsuccessful, she will be sprung on her third turn. Once the princess leaves the Dungeon, she has to return to the Nursery to start the game over.

THE CHAPEL:

Each princess must enter the Chapel. To do so, she must roll an exact number for the remaining spaces—no less, no more. Once she is in the Chapel, the princess rolls another die to choose her fate. An even roll (2, 4, or 6) places her into the holy state of matrimony—she must travel along the Family Path toward the Throne Room. An odd roll (1, 3, or 5) allows the princess to remain without a prince—she must travel along the Good Works Path toward the Throne Room.

THE THRONE ROOM:

To enter the Throne Room and win the game, a princess has to throw an exact number for the remaining spaces—no less, no more. The first princess to get to the Throne Room is crowned queen.

GAME VARIATION:

for more than two players: After the princess has become a queen, enact a coronation ceremony. (A variety of crowns can be downloaded at BadPrincessBook.com.) Each losing player must swear allegiance to the new queen. The player with the most convincing speech will be made heir to the throne.

SELECTED FURTHER READING

If you'd like to learn more about life as a princess, try these:

The Real Princess Diaries by Grace Norwich, published by Scholastic Inc..

Real Princesses: An Inside Look at the Royal Life by Valerie Wilding, published by Walker Books for Young Readers.

Want to read the first fairy tales from way back when? Try these:

The Annotated Hans Christian Andersen by Hans Christian Andersen, with an introduction and notes by Maria Tatar, published by W. W. Norton & Company.

Beauties, Beasts and Enchantment: Classic French Fairy Tales edited and translated by Jack Zipes, published by Crescent Moon Publishing.

The Original Folk and Fairy Tales of the Brothers Grimm: The Complete First Edition by Jacob and Wilhelm Grimm, published by Princeton University Press.

Fascinated by the Tudors? Try these:

Henry VIII: Royal Beheader by Sean Stewart Price, published by Franklin Watts.

Behind the Mask: The Life of Queen Elizabeth I by Jane Resh Thomas, published by Clarion Books.

Finally, some individual princess biographies:

A Princess Found: An American Family, an African Chiefdom, and the Daughter Who Connected Them All by Sarah Culberson and Tracy Trivas, published by St. Martin's Press.

Princess Diana by Joanne Mattern, published by DK Children.

Princess Ka'iulani: Hope of a Nation, Heart of a People by Sharon Linnéa, published by Eerdmans Books for Young Readers.

ACKNOWLEDGMENTS

Books are by their nature a communal effort. Though my name may be on the cover of *Bad Princess*, many people were involved behind the scenes. I am especially appreciative of Paige Hazzan, my wonderful editor at Scholastic, who always understood my vision, and my ever-supportive agent, Michelle Brower. Also at Scholastic, Christopher Stengel and Kay Petronio helped perfect the design, Maeve Norton worked on the beautiful cover, Emily Teresa assisted with photo research, and Maya Frank-Levine made sure production ran smoothly. I am also indebted to Theresa Park, Kristine Puopolo, and Heather Lazare, who provided invaluable feedback during the early development of this book, and to Sandra Gulland for her expertise on all things Louis XIV. A big pink sparkly *merci* to my husband, Thomas Ross Miller, whose insight and scholarship helped *Bad Princess* evolve from a glint in my mind into the book you're now holding. On the art front, I am grateful for the friendship and technical support of Amy Saidens, digital illustrator extraordinaire. Finally, a bouquet of tiaras to the "bad princesses" who gamely posed for the illustrations. They include Michelle Brower, Marci Jefferson, Dalia Kirsenblat, Thea Miller, Kaia Peterson, and Heather Webb—thank you all!

ABOUT THE AUTHOR

Kris Waldherr is the award-winning author and illustrator of *Doomed Queens: Royal Women Who Met Bad Ends*, *The Book of Goddesses*, and other books for children and adults. *The New Yorker* called *Doomed Queens* "utterly satisfying." *The Book of Goddesses* was a One Spirit/Book-of-the-Month Club's Top Ten Most Popular Book. *The New York Times Book Review* praised her picture book *Persephone and the Pomegranate* for its "quality of myth and magic." As a child, Waldherr became fascinated with royalty after her great-aunt revealed their family was distantly related to English nobility.

Kris Waldherr lives in a ghost-ridden Victorian house in Brooklyn with her husband and tween-age daughter, who no longer likes princesses. Learn more at KrisWaldherr.com.